THE LOGOS OF THE SENSIBLE WORLD

THE COLLECTED WRITINGS OF JOHN SALLIS

Volume III/10

THE LOGOS OF THE SENSIBLE WORLD

Merleau-Ponty's Phenomenological Philosophy

John Sallis

Edited by Richard Rojcewicz

Indiana University Press

This book is a publication of

Indiana University Press
Office of Scholarly Publishing
Herman B Wells Library 350
1320 East 10th Street
Bloomington, Indiana 47405 USA

iupress.indiana.edu

Based on the lecture course of 1970–71
at Duquesne University,
with supplementary material from
the lecture course of 1968–69 at Duquesne University.

Manufactured in the United States of America

Cataloging information is available from the Library of Congress.

ISBN 978-0-253-04044-2 (hardback)
ISBN 978-0-253-04045-9 (paperback)
ISBN 978-0-253-04048-0 (ebook)

1 2 3 4 5   24 23 22 21 20 19

Contents

Key to the Citations of Merleau-Ponty's Works

THE WORKS OF Merleau-Ponty will be cited according to the following abbreviations, succeeded by the page number of the published English translation and then of the original. The translations quoted in the text are occasionally modifications of the published ones.

HT: *Humanism and Terror: An Essay on the Communist Problem*, tr. John O'Neill. Boston: Beacon Press, 1969. *Humanisme et terreur: Essai sur le problème communiste*. Paris: Gallimard, 1947.

IP: *In Praise of Philosophy*, tr. John Wild and James Edie. Evanston, IL: Northwestern University Press, 1963. *Éloge de la philosophie*. Paris: Gallimard, 1953.

PP: *Phenomenology of Perception*, tr. Colin Smith. New York: Humanities Press, 1962. *Phénoménologie de la perception*. Paris: Gallimard, 1945.

PR: "The Primacy of Perception," tr. James Edie. In *The Primacy of Perception and Other Essays on Phenomenological Psychology, the Philosophy of Art, History, and Politics*. Evanston, IL: Northwestern University Press, 1964. *Le primat de la perception et ses conséquences philosophiques*. Grenoble: Cynara, 1989. Originally published in the *Bulletin de la société française de philosophie*, Dec. 1947, pp. 119–53.

S: *Signs*, tr. Richard McCleary. Evanston, IL: Northwestern University Press, 1964. *Signes*. Paris: Gallimard, 1960.

SB: *The Structure of Behavior*, tr. Alden Fisher. Boston: Beacon Press, 1963. *La structure du comportement*. Paris: Presses Universitaires de France, 1942.

SN: *Sense and Non-Sense*, tr. Hubert and Patricia Dreyfus. Evanston, IL: Northwestern University Press, 1964. *Sens et non-sens*. Paris: Gallimard, 1948.

TL: *Themes from the Lectures at the Collège de France*, tr. John O'Neill. Evanston, IL: Northwestern University Press, 1970. *Résumés de cours Collège de France 1952–1960*. Paris: Gallimard, 1968.

VI: *The Visible and the Invisible*, tr. Alphonso Lingis. Evanston, IL: Northwestern University Press, 1968. *Le visible et l'invisible*. Paris: Gallimard, 1964.

THE LOGOS OF THE SENSIBLE WORLD

Introduction

"The end of a philosophy is the account of its beginning." So says Merleau-Ponty in one of the "Working Notes" to *The Visible and the Invisible* (VI 177, 231).

If we set out to expound and interpret Merleau-Ponty's philosophy, his statement about end and beginning immediately poses a difficulty. For it means we cannot set out by establishing and justifying the starting point of his thought. We cannot simply set this down and then straightforwardly proceed to unfold his philosophy in terms of a logical development from the starting point.

Merleau-Ponty's philosophy is rather one which moves in a circle and does so in a very profound way. In play here is not the circularity of logical argumentation, the kind of circularity it would be appropriate to want to get rid of. It is rather a circularity arising out of Merleau-Ponty's reflection on the very character of philosophical thought, a circularity which to that extent is akin to the circularity of the Hegelian system and to the hermeneutical circle of Heidegger.

Yet, if we cannot begin by establishing a starting point, it is almost equally inappropriate to begin with a sketch or general outline of Merleau-Ponty's philosophy. The very character of his work is such as to resist the attempt at a summarizing overview. Consider, for example, what Merleau-Ponty says in "The Metaphysical in Man" from *Sense and Non-Sense*: "Metaphysical consciousness has no other objects than those of everyday experience: this world, other people, human history, truth, culture. But instead of taking them as all settled, as consequences with no premises, and as if they were self-evident, it rediscovers their fundamental strangeness to me and the miracle of their appearing. . . . Understood in this way, metaphysics is the opposite of a system" (SN 94, 165–66).

What I want to attempt as an introduction to Merleau-Ponty is thus not an overview of a supposed system of thought. Rather, I want to examine how Merleau-Ponty's work arises out of an engagement with his contemporary historical and philosophical situation and in that way try to obtain a first glimpse of his problematic.

Today it has become almost the fashion to say that philosophers must be engaged, that they must be involved in the contemporary situation, that their thinking must proceed in response to the issues their situation raises for them. Merleau-Ponty is in agreement with this notion of philosophy; one could perhaps even regard the whole of his work as an extended effort to understand the sense of this engagement and the source of its necessity.

At the same time, the result of his work is to refine the notion of engagement, even to the point where it begins to look like something quite different from what we might usually think. Merleau-Ponty comes to see that the engagement of the philosopher is an engagement permeated with ambiguity. It is an engagement which is simultaneously a withdrawal, a disengagement: "One must be able to step back to be capable of true engagement. . . . That the philosopher limps behind is his virtue. True irony is not an alibi; it is a task and is the detachment which assigns the philosopher a certain kind of action among men" (IP 60–61, 70–71). This sort of ambiguous or dialectical engagement is concretely evident in Merleau-Ponty's own career.

Maurice Jean Jacques Merleau-Ponty was born in 1908. He grew up mostly in Paris and was educated at L'École normale supérieure. It was there that he first met Sartre, with whom he was to have an important and lifelong association.

After Merleau-Ponty graduated with the equivalent of an MA in 1930, he spent five years teaching in a lycée, first at Beauvais, then at Chartres. In 1935 he returned to teach at L'École normale. Then the war broke out, and in 1939 he entered the army. During the Occupation he worked (together with Sartre) in the resistance movement and wrote his first two books: *The Structure of Behavior* and *Phenomenology of Perception*.

After the war, he defended those two works to receive his doctorate from L'École normale and became professor at the University of Lyon. In 1950 he came to the Sorbonne as Professor of Psychology and Pedagogy (teaching mainly child psychology). Then in 1952 he was appointed Professor of Philosophy in the Collège de France. The chair to which he was appointed had previously been held by Louis Lavelle and Henri Bergson. It is perhaps the highest philosophical position in France, and Merleau-Ponty was the youngest philosopher ever to occupy it.

The most important document regarding the concrete course of Merleau-Ponty's career is an essay Sartre published in a memorial volume of *Les Temps Modernes* shortly after Merleau-Ponty's death. In this essay Sartre divides Merleau-Ponty's career into three stages:

(1) up to publication of *Phenomenology of Perception* in 1945;
(2) 1945–52: period of political involvement;
(3) 1953–61: return to more strictly philosophical concerns.

Here we see clearly the peculiar interplay of engagement and disengagement characteristic of Merleau-Ponty's work. After the completion of his first two books, there followed a period of intense involvement in politics. During this period Merleau-Ponty wrote little else but occasional essays, ones addressed directly to the social and political issues of postwar Europe. He served during this time as political editor of *Les Temps Modernes*, the left-wing periodical of which

Sartre was officially the editor. It was here that Merleau-Ponty first published most of his extensive political commentaries.

Regarding this period, Sartre later wrote: "His thesis finished, he seemed to have abandoned his investigations in order to interrogate the history and politics of our time." But then Sartre goes on to suggest that Merleau-Ponty's turn to politics was not simply an abandonment of philosophy but was rather an engagement in the concrete historical situation, an engagement required by his philosophy and providing an essential mediation in the unfolding of his work: "He acted in order to appropriate his action and to find himself in depth."

We are reminded here of what Merleau-Ponty wrote at the end of the *Phenomenology of Perception*: "Whether it is a matter of things or historical situations, philosophy has no other function than to allow us to see these things and situations accurately, and so it is true that philosophy consummates itself by destroying itself—as isolated philosophy. But here we must fall silent, for only the hero lives his relations to human beings and to the world all the way to the end, and it is not proper for anyone else to speak in his name" (PP 456, 520).

It is as though Merleau-Ponty, through his first two books, was brought to the limits, the bounds, of theory and thereby was forced into the dimension of praxis.

The story of Merleau-Ponty's political involvement is primarily the story of his relation to Marxism and of the change in that relation. His initial position regarding Marxism was expressed in a series of articles he published in *Les Temps Modernes* in the years immediately following the end of the war. These articles were later published together in the book *Humanism and Terror*. There Merleau-Ponty maintains a distinction between the theoretical level and the practical level. On the theoretical level he expresses a qualified acceptance of Marxism as a philosophy of history. But on the practical level Merleau-Ponty maintains an attitude of "Marxist anticipation." This he relates to the fact that, while the Marxist critique of the West is largely valid, the practice of Marxism in Russia is little better than what preceded, for it has tended to produce a new hierarchical society, a static political regime, and an institutionalizing of terror.

In his view both East and West have failed to live up to their theories, and France, he argues, must remain *between* East and West: "One cannot be anticommunist, one cannot be communist" (HT xxi, 16). Nevertheless, Merleau-Ponty had some hope for Russian communism, and his attitude of "Marxist anticipation" was one of refusing to disapprove of communist politics, in the hope that this politics might eventually evoke a genuine awakening of the proletariat.

Several factors precipitated the change in Merleau-Ponty's attitude to Marxism that occurred around 1950. The decisive break came with the eruption of the Korean War, which, in his opinion, Russia could have prevented. Merleau-Ponty held that the effect of this war was to create two armed camps and to remove the possibility of a third force (namely, France). Merleau-Ponty imposed political silence on *Les Temps Modernes* for two years, and in 1953 he resigned from the periodical after a quarrel with Sartre.

Merleau-Ponty's break with Marxism and with Sartre was announced in 1955 with publication of *Les aventures de la dialectique*, a book which brought a sarcastic rebuttal from Simone de Beauvoir. In this book, Merleau-Ponty expressed total disillusionment with communist politics. Furthermore, he now found the source of these failings in Marx himself, that is, in Marx's movement from humanism to scientific socialism. Merleau-Ponty confessed that his own earlier position, in which he justified Marxism independently of its historical forms, had been a nonhistorical type of thinking. Now he declares that the proletariat as a universal class—about which he had become progressively more skeptical—no longer exists in international politics. Finally, he even argues that there is no longer any reason to think that a revolutionary must be one who believes in overturning all existing institutions; instead, a revolutionary outlook is possible today within a parliamentary framework.

In the last period of his career, Merleau-Ponty withdrew from his intense political engagement. There is reason to believe that this withdrawal was not an arbitrary break but rather that the need for it was generated precisely by the course Merleau-Ponty's engagement had taken.

In any case, he returned after 1953 to the more strictly theoretical concerns characteristic of his first two books. In a sense he undertook now to complete what he had begun. He says in a "Prospectus" published in the *Revue de métaphysique et de morale* the year after he died: "My first two works sought to restore the world of perception. My works in preparation aim to show how communication with others, and thought, take up and go beyond the realm of perception which initiated us to the truth" (PR 3, 401).

Yet, at the same time, Merleau-Ponty displays a vast broadening of perspectives and, most importantly, an attention to the fundamental ontological dimension that had remained uninterrogated in his earlier writings.

The work of this last period was not brought to completion. Merleau-Ponty finished only a few essays before he died suddenly in May 1961. Of the two major books on which he was working, *The Visible and the Invisible* and *The Prose of the World*, we were bequeathed only fragments.

* * *

Merleau-Ponty's work is engaged not only in the sense of an involvement in the concrete social and political movements of his time but also in the sense that Merleau-Ponty understands his own philosophical task from out of the situation brought about by the development of modern philosophy and science.

I want to obtain a first glimpse of his problematic by seeing how his work emerges in relation to the contemporary philosophical situation. Undoubtedly, what is here most decisive for Merleau-Ponty is Hegel's philosophy. More specifically, what is decisive is that which this philosophy represents for Merleau-Ponty with respect to traditional philosophy and also with respect to the condition of philosophy after Hegel.

On the one hand, Merleau-Ponty affirms what Engels had already said and what Heidegger has meditated on most profoundly: Hegel is the end of philosophy, Hegel brings philosophy as it had been conceived since Plato to its fulfillment and conclusion. In a summary of a lecture course given in 1958–59, Merleau-Ponty says: "With Hegel, something comes to an end. After Hegel, there is a philosophical void" (TL 100, 141–42). Merleau-Ponty refers specifically to Marx, Kierkegaard, and Nietzsche, to the fact that they begin from a denial of philosophy, that after Hegel we enter an age of nonphilosophy.

But for Merleau-Ponty there is a monstrous ambiguity in Hegel: he is not only the end but at the same time contains the seeds of a transformation and renewal of philosophy. Speaking of the destruction of philosophy after Hegel, Merleau-Ponty writes: "But perhaps such a destruction of philosophy constitutes its very realization. Perhaps it preserves the essence of philosophy, and it may be, as Husserl wrote, that philosophy is reborn from its own ashes" (TL 100, 142).

The way Hegel contains the seeds of a new philosophical beginning is expressed in the essay "Hegel's Existentialism" from *Sense and Non-Sense*: "Hegel is the origin of everything great in the last hundred years of philosophy: Marxism, Nietzsche, phenomenology, German existentialism, and psychoanalysis. These all go back to Hegel, inasmuch as he began the attempt to explore the irrational and integrate it into an expanded reason which remains the task of our century" (SN 63, 109).

We must try to understand this notion of integrating the irrational into an expanded reason. Note that Merleau-Ponty speaks of an "*expanded* reason" into which the irrational is integrated. This suggests immediately that the new concept of reason is not the narrow concept (for example, the one prevailing in the Enlightenment) which is *simply opposed* to the irrational. Rather, reason is now expanded so as in some way to encompass the irrational, so as to sustain a richer relation to the irrational.

In this connection we can distinguish two possible ways of regarding the integration of the irrational into the rational. These are already broached in the two ways the fateful word *aufheben* can be understood. These two ways correspond roughly to the right-wing and left-wing interpretations of Hegelian thought.

The first ("right-wing") way of interpretation stresses the unity, the reconciliation of the irrational with the rational. Here integration means that the irrational is taken up into the rational such that the irrationality of the irrational is negated, annulled, surpassed. In other words, reason is expanded so as to encompass everything and in such a way that within its scope even the irrational ultimately proves to be rational. Or, to put it differently, the irrational is integrated into the rational such that the tension between the rational and irrational is annulled in favor of rationality.

Let us see, more concretely, what this alternative means with respect to our understanding of man. Most fundamentally, it entails an understanding of the *essence* of man as rationality. That is to say, man is essentially rational: he is an image of the ideal of rationality, of the rational ideal. Thus if, in man, irrationality is always, as a matter of fact, a component, this irrationality is purely negative. It results only from the circumstance that man is never what he *should* be, that he falls short of the rational ideal. Irrationality is accidental, not essential.

Traditionally this rational ideal is understood theologically. Man is an image of the divine but falls short of the divine. Man's task is then to rid himself of this nonessential irrationality and thus become like the divine. Philosophy becomes the practice of dying.

It is not necessary, however, that this way of understanding man be worked out in theological terms. In fact it persists today even where all theology and all Platonic metaphysics are explicitly excluded. What we find after the death of God is that the rational ideal is regarded not as God but as something fabricated by man.

That is, man continues to be understood as essentially rational, as in principle subject to unlimited rationalization, unlimited approximation to an ideal. But this time the ideal is posited by man himself. In the extreme case, man is understood as subject to unlimited technologizing.

I have pursued this interpretation of the Hegelian right, not because it is Merleau-Ponty's interpretation—it obviously is *not*—but rather to bring out certain features of the tradition *against* which Merleau-Ponty's thought is moving. (The opposition of the existentialists to technology, for example, is aimed at an entire tradition, not just at some specific feature of present-day society.)

To this interpretation according to the Hegelian right, Merleau-Ponty opposes an interpretation according to the Hegelian left. If Merleau-Ponty can speak of "Hegel's Existentialism," it is because Hegel's thought contains another possibility opposed to the one we have just traced out.

So there is a second way of understanding the integration of the irrational into the rational: we can understand it as an integration in which the irrational is preserved rather than annulled. That means we can understand the integration as one which does not dissolve the irrational but rather transforms the rational by bringing it into an essential relation with the irrational. More specifically, we can understand the integration as one in which reason is carried back to its *rootedness* in an opaque and irreducible irrational or pre-rational dimension.

What does this general alternative entail with respect to the concept of man? Toward the middle of *In Praise of Philosophy*, Merleau-Ponty writes: "The discord of man with himself, which up to now impeded him from being the 'divine man,' now constitutes his reality and his value. He is divided because he is not a 'species' or a 'created thing,' because he is a 'creative effort'" (IP 27, 35).

Here Merleau-Ponty is referring to a *discord* of man with himself, an irrationality in man, a tension within man between the rational and the irrational. This irrationality, according to Merleau-Ponty, has previously been conceived as that which separates man from the divine: it has been conceived negatively. In turn, man's task was to eliminate this factor so as to imitate the divine.

But Merleau-Ponty wants to reverse this way of thought and take this irrationality and discord *positively*, as positively constitutive of the nature of man. Man is not a "created thing," an image of a divine archetype. He is not something whose essence is realized in an unlimited approximation to the divine, to a rational ideal. He is rather a "creative effort."

What this means (man as *creative* effort) is that man is to be understood as the *locus* of the interplay of the rational and pre-rational, *and*, in turn, this interplay is *not* to be regarded as dictated or prescribed by some metaphysical ideal. In other words, man is regarded as the place where meaning emerges from out of a background which is pre-meaningful and which remains obscure, opaque, concealed. Merleau-Ponty says that man is condemned to meaning: man is condemned to be the place of the emergence of meaning.

It is crucial to Merleau-Ponty's thought that this emergence of meaning is *essentially finite*. My concepts and language, my way of understanding the world, always remain rooted in something pre-conceptual, specifically in the pre-theoretical presence of the world to me. Whatever emerges into the clear light of rationality is necessarily set against a background which is opaque, pre-rational.

It is because human existence is so situated, because it is the locus of a finite emergence of meaning, that it is—to use Merleau-Ponty's word—*ambiguous*. *In Praise of Philosophy* offers several characterizations of this ambiguity of the human situation:

> The relation of the philosopher to being is not the frontal relation of the spectator to the spectacle; it is a kind of complicity, an oblique and clandestine relation. (IP 15, 22)

> Our relation with being involves a double sense, the first according to which we belong to it, the second according to which it belongs to us. (IP 5, 11)

> Philosophy cannot be a tête-à-tête of the philosopher with the truth. It cannot be a judgment given from on high regarding life, the world, history, as if the philosopher were not part of it. (IP 30, 38)

Man is always already a part of it; he is always already in the world and history. Consequently, whenever he comes to engage in knowledge or action he does so from out of an already established presence to the world and to history, and his action and knowledge are to this degree always permeated with ambiguity:

Action always takes place against a background in which I am already immersed and which can never be made perfectly transparent. I act from out of a tradition which surpasses me as an individual, and in acting I help found a tradition which likewise surpasses me and my particular intentions.

And as regards knowledge, I am unable to withdraw myself from the world in such a way as to gain a view of the world "from the outside." Rather, I am always already *in the world*, and if I come to conceptualize the world I can do so only from the vantage point of the anchorage I already have in the world.

Now we can begin to see vaguely the primary articulations of Merleau-Ponty's work.

His first writings are devoted to the interrogation of this pre-rational anchorage in the world. The entire issue is crystallized and developed in terms of the thesis of the primacy of perception. But, once this interrogation is complete, Merleau-Ponty's task becomes that of carrying reason back to its rootedness in the pre-rational domain of perceptual experience. In other words, his phenomenology of perception brings him finally to the question of the origin of truth, to the question of *logos*.

And if, with Heraclitus, philosophy itself has its origins in a listening to the *logos*, if, as Merleau-Ponty says with an obvious allusion to Heidegger, it is a matter of Being speaking within us, then we see that the problem of *logos* is simultaneously the problem of the nature of philosophy itself. And we start to see how it is that the end of a philosophy is the account of its beginning.

I. The Structure of Behavior

A. Introduction

We situated Merleau-Ponty's work with respect to Hegel and suggested that Merleau-Ponty tries to bring to fruition the seeds of the new beginning that are contained in Hegel. In this connection we considered Merleau-Ponty's description of the contemporary philosophical task as that of exploring the irrational and integrating it into an expanded reason.

We tried then to grasp the more specific form this task assumes for Merleau-Ponty. We saw that there are two primary issues: that of exploring our pre-rational anchorage in the world and that of reestablishing the connection of reason with this anchorage. It is to the former of these issues that Merleau-Ponty's first two books are primarily directed.

We now need to gain some idea of what is at issue in this question of man's pre-rational anchorage so as to see why Merleau-Ponty's treatment of the question assumes the form it does.

In traditional terms, to speak of man's anchorage in the world means to speak about the relation of subject and object, about the relation of consciousness to nature. At the beginning of *The Structure of Behavior*, Merleau-Ponty formulates his problem in precisely that way: "Our goal is to understand the relations of consciousness and nature" (SB 3, 1).

It is essential to see, however, what form this understanding will take. In effect, Merleau-Ponty will show that the subject-object relation, as it is usually conceived, is a *founded relation*. That is, he will show that beneath the level at which consciousness stands over against an object, there is an already established anchorage, a primordial contact between man and world.

In other words, Merleau-Ponty's intention is not simply to explicate the relation of consciousness to nature but rather to penetrate beneath it to a dimension which is always already presupposed, always already established, but for the most part is forgotten, covered over by the natural attitude. It is in this connection that Merleau-Ponty takes up the work of Husserl and thus understands his own work as "phenomenology." Especially in the later genetic phenomenology of Husserl, Merleau-Ponty sees a return to origins and takes up Husserl's fundamental distinction between the predicative and the pre-predicative, between passive genesis and active genesis, between a level of explicit, conscious, judgmental activity and an already presupposed substratum by which we are always already in contact with a world, by which a world is always already there for us. As Merleau-Ponty says regarding phenomenology at the beginning of the *Phenomenology of Perception*: "For phenomenology the world is always 'already there,' prior to reflection, as an incontrovertible presence. Phenomenology even directs all its effort toward rejoining this naive contact with the world and granting it, finally, philosophical status" (PP vii, i).

Merleau-Ponty's first works are an attempt to explore this pre-predicative dimension, to explore this "lifeworld." In general, he understands this dimension as being the domain of perceptual experience, as we saw in his "Prospectus": "My first two works sought to restore the world of perception." And, following Husserl, his exploration takes the form of a phenomenology; thus a description, not an explanation or analysis.

So Merleau-Ponty's task is that of a phenomenology of perception. Nevertheless, his first work is not this phenomenology but a book about behavior as such. We need to see what Merleau-Ponty undertakes in this book, why it was necessary for him to do so, and how *The Structure of Behavior* is related to Merleau-Ponty's overall philosophical task.

Merleau-Ponty wants to execute a regress beneath the level of the subject-object relation to the level of perceptual experience already presupposed. In other words, Merleau-Ponty wants to execute a phenomenological reduction by which he can get beneath the natural attitude. He wants to suspend the natural attitude which takes the subject-object relation for granted so that he can open up, beneath this, the genuinely primordial dimension.

What eventually proves to be especially characteristic of this primordial dimension is its peculiar *holistic* character. That means it is a dimension wherein all the distinctions which seem so obvious and clear to the natural attitude are blurred. It is a dimension in which the dichotomies appearing on the level of subject and object collapse, a dimension in which all elements are "intertwined."

More specifically, within this dimension, the subject and the object are seen to be moments of a whole, a totality, rather than two distinct things related either by the causality of objects or by the constitutive power of the subject. Objects can no longer be regarded as so many discrete things in themselves linked only by causal connections. Instead, they must be regarded as showing themselves only within the context of a whole, only from out of a world. And the subject can no longer be understood as a pure consciousness linked externally to a body. Rather, consciousness and body now appear as intertwined, such that we must speak of a lived-body, a body-subject, and of consciousness precisely as bodily, as incarnate. Yet none of this is evident to the natural attitude, which remains at the level of the subject-object relation. Hence, in order to make this dimension accessible and to open up the field of a phenomenology of perception, Merleau-Ponty must suspend the natural attitude.

He does so, however, not by simply bypassing the natural attitude but rather by moving through it. More specifically, he moves not just through the natural attitude but also through the scientific positions of naturalism or empiricism in which the natural attitude has its most accentuated form—thus through empirical psychology and the naturalistic conception of the relation of consciousness to nature.

What is the character of this movement? It amounts to Merleau-Ponty showing that there are scientifically established facts which cannot be accounted for by empiricism. That means he takes up, at the level of scientific research, the problems of scientific psychology in order to demonstrate that the scientific findings are irreconcilable with the fundamental presuppositions of naturalism.

It is important to understand what kind of enterprise this is. It is neither a mere critique of scientific theories *nor*, strictly speaking, a philosophical or phenomenological critique of science, an attack on science from a certain philosophical position. Rather than taking up a point of view outside of science, Merleau-Ponty places his inquiry within science in order to turn scientific psychology against itself or, in other words, in order to expose *by the very method of science* the inadequacies of the naturalistic presuppositions of psychology.

But, in this, there is a philosophical motive, and thus it is no mere critique of science: what Merleau-Ponty wants to show is the necessity of going beyond naturalism, the necessity of forging new fundamental concepts geared to a more fundamental dimension than that of the subject-object relation. In effect, Merleau-Ponty suspends the natural attitude, in the form of naturalism, by making it collapse under the weight of its own findings, by making it *suspend itself.* Accordingly, *The Structure of Behavior* is Merleau-Ponty's way of *executing the phenomenological reduction.*

* * *

One might well ask why such a circuitous route is necessary. Why is it not sufficient simply to set the natural attitude as such out of action? Why is it necessary to make this detour through empirical psychology?

There are two reasons:

First, it provides a way of avoiding a dilemma which often plagued Husserl, namely, the problem of the motivation of the phenomenological reduction. The problem is this: if I suspend the natural attitude, I do so because I somehow realize its inadequacy; otherwise, I would simply remain within it. But how do I realize its inadequacy? Certainly that inadequacy is evident once I have suspended the natural attitude in favor of the transcendental standpoint, but it must in some way also be evident before the suspension, or else I would not be led to suspend it in the first place.

Merleau-Ponty's procedure shows how the natural attitude is able to reveal its inadequacy without our having already suspended it in favor of a higher standpoint. What he shows is that its inadequacies become evident when it is extended and accentuated in the form of empirical psychology.

But there is a more important reason for the detour through naturalism: there is a "truth of naturalism." There is a truth brought to light by naturalism which needs to be preserved, which needs to be purified and carried over into transcendental philosophy. What is this truth? It is the dependence, the rootedness, of mind, of consciousness, in the world and especially in the body. Naturalistic psychology (behaviorism) distorts this truth when it reduces consciousness to the level of the body taken as a physical object, and Merleau-Ponty indeed wants to expose this distortion. On the other hand, transcendental philosophy is simply ignoring this truth when it separates the subject as pure consciousness from the body. (Especially in the *Phenomenology of Perception*, Merleau-Ponty will devote a great deal of effort to confronting transcendental philosophy with this "truth of naturalism," which his first work releases from its naturalistic presuppositions.)

Merleau-Ponty, in opposition both to empiricism and to transcendental philosophy, wants to relativize the distinction between consciousness and body. Hence, he chooses to thematize behavior, which is neither purely mental nor purely physical. Rather than conceiving consciousness either as reducible to the body or as something totally distinct and externally imposed on the body, Merleau-Ponty wants to understand consciousness as a structure which emerges from bodily existence but which also has its own originality (and is not reducible to the bodily).

That is possible only if the body is to some degree homogenous with consciousness, only if within bodily existence there is already prefigured the kind of structure characteristic of consciousness. And this requires, in particular, that the body no longer be regarded as just another physical object, as something in-itself, as a mere thing.

On the negative side, *The Structure of Behavior* attempts to show that such a conception of the body cannot be maintained. It does so by focusing on the two primary features of the empiricist's concept of the body which rob it of its affinity with consciousness and which stand in the way of conceiving an internal connection between the body and consciousness.

(1) The body as *passive* in experience: this empiricist precept is evident specifically in the behavioristic notion of the body as a cluster of anatomical structures. Each of these structures is regarded as consisting of a receptor connected through a reflex arc to an effector in such a way that the response—rather than being actively elaborated by the organism—is completely determined by the stimulus and the preestablished anatomy.

(2) The body as *atomistic* ("parts outside of parts"): this means that both the excitation and the response are regarded as mere sums and that there is no allowance for wholes that would be more than a mere sum of parts.

On the positive side, *The Structure of Behavior* prepares the way for a new conception of the body according to which the rootedness of conscious existence in bodily existence can be made intelligible. In other words, it prepares the way for a concept of the body whereby the "truth of naturalism" can be purified and preserved.

B. Chapter 1 of *The Structure of Behavior*: Reflex Behavior

a.) The Classical Theory

The classical theory of behavior is based on the simple idea of a reflex.

stimulus ⟶ receptor   reflex circuit   effector ⟶ reaction

This process is taken to be the basic unit of behavior. The physiologist's task is to explain complex behavior in terms of such units. The explanation runs as follows. Complex excitation is resolvable into a sum of discrete stimuli, each of which acts on a discrete receptor. The impulse arising at the receptor is in each case carried through the circuit—independently of what is happening in other circuits—to the effector, where it produces a response. The sum of these discrete responses constitutes the total complex response.

Merleau-Ponty calls attention to important consequences of this theory:

(1) The whole process is one of mutual exteriority of parts. Behavior is regarded as a mere sum of independent atomic units, each nerve circuit being isolated from the others. That is to say, this theory construes behavior *atomistically.*

(2) As a result, formal properties such a movement, rhythm, and spatial arrangement cannot affect the organism. Form—since it pertains to the whole—is not registered. All that is registered is a mere sum of pointlike stimulations external to one another. Thus the stimulus can act only by those of its properties that can affect the receptors taken one by one.

(3) The relation between excitation and response is understood as *passive*, that is, understood solely in terms of preestablished anatomical connections. The organism is passive "since it limits itself to executing what is prescribed for it by the place of the excitation and by the nerve circuits which originate there" (SB 9, 7). Topography is primary.

(4) This theory eliminates all notions of intention, utility, or value from behavior. These are banished as something merely subjective. For example, if I reach for an object, it is not because I apprehend the object as endowed with

possible use or value for me but rather because certain physical stimuli (light waves) have acted on certain receptors.

b.) Critique of the Classical Theory

Merleau-Ponty's critique proceeds by examining the various components of the reflex: stimulus, place of excitation, reflex circuit, reaction. In each case he draws on experimental findings in order to show the inadequacy of the classical conception. Here Merleau-Ponty appeals mostly to the work of Kurt Goldstein (*The Organism*).

I will summarize and will deal with only a few of the experimental results with regard to:

(1) The stimulus.
(2) The place of excitation.
(3) The reflex circuit.
(4) The reaction.

(1) The stimulus.

To the classical concept Merleau-Ponty opposes the fact that the *form* of the stimulus influences the response and hence plays a role in determining the character of the stimulus as stimulus. Merleau-Ponty cites instances in which the response is made to vary simply by varying the form and also instances in which the content of the stimulus is varied while the form remains constant, with the result that the response does not vary. Thus form, that which makes a complex stimulus other than a mere sum of its elements, must in some way be registered in the organism, since form influences the response.

But it is not sufficient just to maintain that the organism receives the form, perhaps the same way a keyboard receives form. Rather, the organism itself must be conceived as contributing to the constitution of that form. Merleau-Ponty gives this example:

> When my hand follows each effort of a struggling animal while I hold an instrument for capturing it, it is clear that each of my movements responds to an external stimulation; but it is also clear that these stimulations could not be received without the movements by which I expose my receptors to their influence. The properties of the object and the intentions of the subject are not only intermingled; they also constitute a new whole. When the eye follows an animal in flight, it is impossible to say "which started first" in the exchange of stimuli and responses. (SB 13, 11)

But if the organism contributes to the constitution of the form of a complex stimulus—and all the stimuli we know of are complex—then the stimulus cannot be defined in itself independently of the organism. Instead, the stimulus already involves the organism, already embodies a *response*. (Here Merleau-Ponty points to the fact that in describing stimuli we inevitably do so in terms of the response: we speak of a "painful stimulus.")

It is thus apparent that Merleau-Ponty is rejecting at the level of the stimulus those two features of the classical theory which stand in the way of bringing together consciousness and the body: atomicity and passivity. A complex stimulus is not a mere sum of parts. Instead, the form, the characteristics that pertain to the stimulus as a whole, must be taken into account. Also, the organism is not passive in such a way that the stimulus merely impinges on it. Instead, the organism is active in that it contributes to the constitution of the stimulus.

(2) Place of excitation.

Here Merleau-Ponty's argument is straightforward. According to the classical theory, the receptor (the place of excitation) should strictly determine the response. But it is not so. Merleau-Ponty cites data showing that excitation of the same receptor can, under certain circumstances, produce completely different reactions. Thus, it is impossible to establish a simple one-to-one relation between receptor and response.

(3) The reflex circuit.

Merleau-Ponty raises this question: is there, in fact, a defined and isolated pathway running from the excitation to the reaction, from receptor to effector?

Merleau-Ponty points out an established fact that there are no reflexes of such a character as to be affected only by external stimuli. Rather, as Goldstein has demonstrated, *all* reflexes depend on a number of conditions in the organism but external to the reflect circuit itself. To this extent the circuit is not purely isolated.

There are various chemical conditions which, if instituted in the organism, can cancel, sometimes even reverse, the usual response to a certain stimulus. Reflexes are also subject to various cerebral and cerebellar influences. For example, shock can modify virtually all the reflexes. And in humans, even paying attention to a reflex is often sufficient to inhibit it.

The problem thus becomes how to retain the notion of preestablished pathways and yet account for these various influences outside the reflex circuit. The usual way of solving this has been to introduce a hierarchical structure of two levels into the nervous system: at the first level are reflex circuits and, at the second level, there is cerebral activity which merely coordinates and associates the preestablished reflex circuits.

Merleau-Ponty attacks this solution with a mass of experimental data. In general, what he demonstrates is that such a solution would involve an almost endless multiplication of hypotheses. Then he presents evidence indicating that cerebral influence is *not* simply a matter of associating and dissociating preestablished circuits. In other words, there is no such simple dualism in the nervous system.

More specifically, the proposed solution involves two difficulties. First, Merleau-Ponty considers a concrete instance of this type of explanation. It is a fact that the plantar flexion reflex (exhibited in the normal subject) is replaced by an extension reflex in the case of a lesion of the pyramidal tracts in the brain. Sherrington's explanation is as follows: in the normal subject the extension reflex which is ready to function is inhibited by excitations from the pyramidal tract; with lesion of the pyramidal tracts, this extension reflex is "set free." But such an explanation is, Merleau-Ponty argues, mere construction for the sake of saving the classical theory: "But this hypothesis cannot be substantiated: the existence of a reflex device which can in no way be observed in the adult and normal subject is posited in order to explain its appearance in the affected subject by a simple 'escape from control'" (SB 19, 18).

Furthermore, the same substitution has been observed in cases where there was no brain damage, and so Sherrington would have to introduce additional hypotheses. And even further, such explanation makes the highly questionable assumption that pathological behavior is to be understood as a mere subtraction from normal behavior, that illness is mere deficit.

There is also another, much simpler difficulty: if above the level of the reflexes we posit a level of cerebral regulation, then this regulation must itself be explained. But how is such explanation possible?

So Merleau-Ponty concludes that cerebral influence does not simply associate and dissociate preestablished devices. There is no simple dualism in the nervous system. Instead, the evidence shows that the effect of cerebral influences is to reorganize behavior as a whole: the central nervous system is the place in which a total image of the organism is elaborated, and this image governs the distribution of the responses and even has an influence on the constitution of the reflex paths.

(4) The reaction.

Merleau-Ponty charges that the classical theory cannot explain the adaptability of the reflex. For example, a reflex movement of scratching depends on the initial position of the effector (the hand) which, of course, is variable. In order to explain this it would be necessary to complicate greatly the simple reflex schema: we would have to suppose that there are as many preestablished circuits at the point to be scratched as there are possible initial positions of the hand.

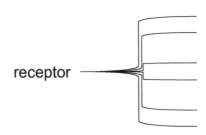

receptor

But then the question becomes: what is there to guarantee that the impulse "chooses" the correct pathway, the one corresponding to the actual position of the hand? Against the usual way of explanation (in terms of another circuit carrying a message which indicates the position of the hand and links up with the original circuit), Merleau-Ponty presents contrary experimental evidence. He then concludes that "the reflex carries within itself the conditions of a correct movement of localization" (SB 29, 28–29).

Thus, in the reaction, as in the other components, the order and coherence of behavior are not based on preestablished anatomical structures such as the classical reflex circuit: "The body in its functioning cannot be defined as a blind mechanism, a mosaic of independent causal sequences" (SB 30, 30). So the obvious question arises: what then is the source of the order and coherence of behavior?

c.) The Reflex in Gestalt Theory

Merleau-Ponty has shown that the relation between stimulus and response is not simply that of a preestablished anatomical structure. The classical theory is not, for example, able to explain the flexibility and adaptiveness of the reflex (such as the one of scratching). So the question arises: is there another way of accounting for the connection between motor reaction and complex stimulus which is not—versus the classical theory—so rigid as to exclude the possibility of adaptiveness?

Merleau-Ponty's answer is inspired by Gestalt psychology, and the key concept is that of equilibrium. According to the Gestalt view, the sensory and motor functions are parts of a unified whole. This was already suggested by the impossibility of distinguishing a stimulus-in-itself. The stimulus already involves a response for its very constitution (example of trying to capture a struggling animal). Within this interconnected whole, each of the two functions (sensory and motor) plays a distinctive role. Motor functions are the means of reestablishing a certain state of equilibrium. Sensory functions provide the conditions necessary for this reestablishment.

Accordingly, the stimulus is connected to the response, not primarily through some preestablished anatomical structure, but rather through the immanence in reflex behavior of certain preferred states of equilibrium to which the stimulus and response are functionally connected. These states of equilibrium constitute objective values of the organism. The stimulus expresses the deviation from equilibrium; the response represents a reorganization by which the equilibrium is reestablished. Merleau-Ponty explains as follows:

> We should consider the afferent sector of the nervous system as a field of forces which express concurrently the intraorganic state and the influence of external agents; these forces tend toward equilibrium according to

certain preferred modes of distribution and obtain from the mobile parts of the body the movements proper to this effect. These movements, as they are executed, provoke modifications in the state of the afferent system which in their turn evoke new movements. This dynamic and circular process would assure the flexible regulation needed in order to account for effective behavior. (SB 46, 48–49)

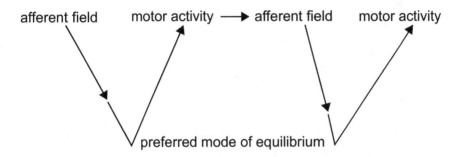

These states of equilibrium = objective values of the organism

Merleau-Ponty presents a number of examples to support and illustrate his theory. For one, it is known that reflex movements of our eyes are such as to allow the eye to receive the richest possible stimulation from the object looked at. Here the preferred state of equilibrium is that of maximum stimulation. The condition for this is given in the visual stimulus (for example, the appearance in the dark of a luminous zone on the periphery of the visual field, which hence is unbalanced in relation to the preferred state of equilibrium). The reflex movement of the eye toward the luminous spot tends to establish this preferred state.

Merleau-Ponty also refers to the reflex movement of the head toward a source of sound. He argues that operative here is a preferred state of equilibrium (that in which the sound would reach both ears simultaneously) and that it is toward establishing this state that the response (turning the head) is directed.

He also mentions some other, more extreme examples. We have seen that the classical theory, with its notion of preestablished anatomical structures, is unable to account for the adaptiveness of reflex behavior to the situation. Merleau-Ponty, on the contrary, argues that the configuration of reflex circuits, rather than being anatomically determined, is subordinated to the maintenance of certain preferred states of equilibrium.

One example concerns transplantation experiments on monkeys. Nerve fibers that ordinarily govern external muscles of monkeys' eyeballs were connected to internal muscles, and vice versa. The monkey is placed in a dark room and a luminous spot is made to appear. The reflex movement of the eyes takes place just as accurately as it did before the nerve fibers were transplanted.

What has happened here? After the disruption of normal anatomic connections, there has occurred a redistribution of function for the new anatomical situation in such way as to maintain a certain mode of behavior. If the anatomical devices were absolutely decisive, if each were absolutely fixed with respect to its function, this could not occur. On the contrary, we would expect a disruption of the reflex movement of the eyes.

The example of hemianopsia represents a most extreme case of adaption, a case in which one set of anatomical devices simply takes over the function normally performed by other such devices. In hemianopsia (investigated by Goldstein) either the right half or left half of each retina is completely insensitive to light—hence the person has the use of only the remaining half of each retina. One would then expect the field of vision of the affected person to correspond to half of the normal field of view. But that is not the case. Instead, the person sees poorly, but his visual field is not reduced to half.

What happens is that the organism adapts itself to the new situation by reorganizing the functions of the eye and in doing so reestablishes equilibrium. That is borne out by Goldstein's observations: the eyeballs oscillate so that the preserved part of the retina is now in the central position, and this, of course, involves a total reorganization of muscular functioning.

Perhaps most remarkably, the various points on the retina do not retain the characteristics they possessed previously. Instead, there is a redistribution. For instance, the point which previously was the fovea and which is now situated on the periphery of the sensitive half of the retina has completely lost its character of being the point of most acute vision and has been replaced by a new "fovea" situated in the center of the sensitive half of the retina.

Merleau-Ponty sums up the import of this example:

> If we adhere to the classical conceptions which relate the perceptual functions of each point of the retina to its anatomical structure—for, example, to the proportion of cones and rods located there—the functional reorganization in hemianopsia is not comprehensible. It becomes so only if the properties of each retinal point are assigned to it, not according to the established local devices, but according to a flexible process of distribution comparable to the division of forces in a drop of oil suspended in water. (SB 41, 42–43)

The point is this: such adaptiveness would be unintelligible if function were strictly prescribed by anatomy. Merleau-Ponty, on the contrary, argues that such extreme cases of adaptiveness are intelligible only in terms of a subordination of anatomical devices to the global task of maintaining or establishing certain preferred states of equilibrium.

d.) Conclusion

Merleau-Ponty concludes by insisting on the necessity of introducing a new category in order to understand behavior, namely, the category of form. (He is using the French word *forme* as the customary translation of the German *Gestalt*. In English, we leave the latter untranslated, and so we can substitute "Gestalt" for "form" in this context.)

In opposition to atomism, Merleau-Ponty has shown how the concept of a whole is necessary. Now he wants to specify the precise kind of concept of wholeness that must be employed. This specific type of whole is designated by the term "form" (or "Gestalt").

We can easily distinguish between two types of wholes. They correspond to the two ways the properties of a whole can depend on the parts.

First, the properties of the whole can depend simply on the properties of the individual parts. Here a property of the whole is merely the sum of the properties of the parts. For example, the weight of a collection of material objects is the sum of the weights of the individual objects. This concept of whole is the only one allowed by the empiricist. Hence, for him, the reflex is a sum of its constituents (stimulus, reaction, etc.), and a complex stimulus is a mere sum of the atomic stimuli. Merleau-Ponty, on the contrary, has tried to show the inadequacy of this concept of whole for understanding behavior.

Second, the properties of the whole may depend on the *relations* among the parts. In such a case, the whole remains the same as long as these relations remain unchanged, regardless of what happens to the individual parts.

Accordingly, if an individual part changes, there are two possible outcomes. If the other remain unchanged, then the whole is changed (since a change in one part alters its relation to the others). If the other parts change in such a way as to preserve the same relations among the parts, then the character of the whole remains unchanged. Example: $\{2, 4, 6\} \rightarrow \{3, 6, 9\}$.

Such wholes, which as wholes are identical although their parts are all different, are called *transposable wholes*. It is this character of a whole which Merleau-Ponty has in mind in speaking of the maintenance of equilibrium. And it is in terms of this concept of whole as form (or Gestalt) that Merleau-Ponty proposes to understand behavior. This is necessary because "in the nervous system there are only global events" (SB 50, 54).

And so we must reject the atomistic presuppositions of empiricism: we must "renounce all types of causal thought" (SB 51, 54).

C. Chapter 2 of *The Structure of Behavior*: Higher Forms of Behavior

WE NEED TO get our bearings—*philosophically*—before we proceed to Chapter 2. It repeats Chapter 1 at a higher level of complexity, but the philosophical necessity of this repetition is not obvious. We could easily lose sight of the philosophical problematic because of the richness of detail in the psychological argumentation and experimentation.

Recall the two main issues of Chapter 1. The first issue is a critique of the classical reflex theory (behaviorism), especially of its fundamental presuppositions, namely, passivity and atomism. In opposition, Merleau-Ponty brings out the constitutive role of the organism and the holistic character of reflex behavior. These are then developed in the notion of equilibrium, which is the second main issue. The notion of equilibrium connects the stimulus and response by subordinating them to a whole and involves both the organism and the situation.

Obviously, the question becomes: how is this equilibrium to be understood? Is it a physiological reality, to be understood causally by decomposition into its elements? In other words, is it to be understood in terms appropriate to a thing? Or is it to be understood through the introduction of the concept of consciousness? In other words, is it to be understood as a regulating idea which consciousness imposes on the level of reflex behavior? In short, does equilibrium have the mode of being of consciousness or of things? Or is there perhaps another alternative?

Chapter 1 does not fully settle this question. It speaks of the necessity of renouncing all types of causal thought. Presumably that excludes understanding equilibrium as a thing. But what is the positive meaning?

In any case, Chapter 1 does help to clarify the issue by generalizing the notion of equilibrium into that of form or Gestalt. Yet, this notion has so far remained abstract, and therefore Chapter 1 must be seen as merely preliminary. It is not evident how this notion can be used to thematize behavior nor what sense is to be given to it ontologically.

What Merleau-Ponty finds necessary is a *repetition* of Chapter 1—but at a level of complexity sufficient to allow the character of form or Gestalt to emerge.

In Chapter 1 Merleau-Ponty developed a critique of the empiricist's account of simple reflex behavior, a critique directed primarily at the three components of the reflex: stimulus, reflex circuit, and response. Now he places himself at the level of "higher forms of behavior," that is, at the level of reflex theory as enriched by the concept of conditioning. Again Merleau-Ponty criticizes the three principal components:

First, the stimulus. Included in the discussion is now the stimulus to which the organism has been conditioned. Hence the critique of Pavlov's theory.

Second, the reflex circuit. The earlier discussion of it led to the problem of regulation by the brain. Hence, now the issue of the "central sector."

Third, the response. The crucial question was that of adaptation. So now Merleau-Ponty will consider that type of reaction in which adaptation is most apparent, namely, learning. Hence the issue of the "structures of behavior."

a.) Pavlov

Pavlov's problem is to explain how it is possible for an organism to enter into relation with a richer and more extensive environment than would seem to be allowed by the reflex connections with which the organism is endowed. Pavlov must explain how the organism is able to multiply the stock of stimuli to which it is sensitive. Thus he must explain how something to which the organism does not originally respond by means of innate anatomical circuits can become for the organism a stimulus calling forth a definite response.

Pavlov attempts this explanation by introducing the notion of a transfer of the power of natural stimuli to new stimuli. This is the concept of the conditioned reflex. It supposes that when a new stimulus acts on an organism, along with another stimulus to which there is a natural response, the new stimulus tends to acquire the reflexogenic power of the natural stimulus. That is, it comes to produce the same response. Thus the new stimulus is brought within the scope of the reflex behavior of the organism. As Merleau-Ponty says: "It is only a question of multiplying the commands on which our inborn reactions depend" (SB 52, 55).

The process by which a new stimulus is connected with the reaction is conditioning. Such an established reflex is the conditioned reflex. The original reflex is then termed the unconditioned reflex. (The classic example is, of course, Pavlov's salivating dog.)

Granting this general theory, then the problem to be solved is that of the direction, adjustment, and selectivity of conditioning. According to the simple schema, conditioning ought to take place, so to speak, in all directions and entirely accidentally. Any stimulus whatsoever which happened to be contiguous with the unconditioned stimulus should get conditioned. Furthermore, once a stimulus is conditioned, it should in turn be able to transfer its reflexogenic power to still another contiguous stimulus even though this latter stimulus may never have been associated with the original unconditioned stimulus. Thus there would be a totally undirected and unstructured proliferation of conditioning.

But that is *not* what happens. Suppose a luminous stimulus L has been conditioned by association with food (the unconditioned stimulus). L alone is then sufficient to make the dog salivate. When we then associate a sound S with L (even though S has not been associated with food), we would expect S to take on the reflexogenic power of L. But what happens is that after a certain period of time, while L alone produces the reaction, L + S produces no response.

Pavlov tries to explain this result by introducing alongside his concept of the conditioned reflex a concept of *conditioned inhibition* by which one stimulus is able to cancel the reflexogenic power of another if presented along with it. But if we consider more complex situations where many different stimuli are involved and are manipulated in various ways, then further anomalies arise, and Pavlov has to introduce further powers (such as counterinhibition) in order to make his theory conform to what is observed.

Merleau-Ponty directs three criticisms at Pavlov's theory:

(1) The theory encounters anomalies, cases with do not fit the schema. Yet in a sense such anomalies are not decisive, for Pavlov can always posit another counterforce so as to correct the result. Thus the question is not whether there are irresolvable anomalies but rather whether we do not have here the old vice of the theorist: a proliferation of auxiliary hypotheses in order to make the original hypothesis fit the facts, as in Ptolemaic astronomy. According to Merleau-Ponty: "A theory which, without experimental support, posits forces in contrary directions obviously escapes being contradicted by experience since it can always bring into play at the right moment one of the two principles in default of the other. For the same reason it is not capable of any experimental justification" (SB 59, 63).

(2) Merleau-Ponty attacks the basic presupposition of Pavlov's theory and suggests that it is this presupposition which makes the proliferation of forces and counterforces necessary. The presupposition is that the total stimulus is to be regarded as a *mere sum* of partial stimuli. The effect of a group of stimuli is then taken as the algebraic sum of the effects of each taken separately, so that in a given case all that is required is to add up the various positive and negative components.

This amounts to assuming that the total stimulus is a whole only in the sense of a sum. The atomistic conception remains just as operative here as in the simple reflex theory. In opposition, Merleau-Ponty insists that "A given objective stimulus produces different effects in the organism depending on whether it acts alone or along with this or that other stimulus. . . . Thus, the genuine stimulus is the ensemble as such" (SB 55, 58–59).

(3) Merleau-Ponty poses the question of the possibility of a *physiological account* of behavior. He argues, specifically, that Pavlov's is *not* a physiological account. Instead, Pavlov uses concepts like excitation, inhibition, and

counterinhibition: concepts which designate, not observed facts, but rather certain *descriptive aspects* of behavior: "Because he carried descriptive notions found in the observation of behavior directly over into the central nervous system, Pavlov was able to believe he employed a physiological method. In reality it amounts to an imaginary physiology. . . . Since no one can in fact start with physiology, Pavlov begins with a study of behavior, with a description of the reactions of the organism in the presence of certain situations—in spite of his own principles" (SB 59–60, 63–64).

What does the discussion of Pavlov's theory accomplish with respect to the *philosophical* issues? In the first place, it shows more pointedly the necessity of introducing a new concept of a whole (form, Gestalt) in place of the empiricist's concept.

But does it clarify the status of form? Does it contribute to answering the question with which we began? In a sense it does—not by answering the question but by indicating a further dimension of the question. By raising the question of the possibility of a physiological account, Merleau-Ponty expands the problematic so that it concerns not only the organism whose behavior is observed but also its way of being present to the observer. In other words, it is a question not only of the mode of being of behavior or of form but also of the way in which behavior presents itself to the observer in the first place and hence makes it possible to thematize behavior and to raise questions such as that of its mode of being.

Merleau-Ponty suggests this "way of presence" is such that the appropriate concepts with which to thematize behavior are descriptive rather than physiological.

b.) The Central Sector

stimulus ⟶ receptor   effector ⟶ reaction

Investigation of reflex behavior (Chapter 1) showed that a reflex circuit is not a self-contained (isolated) unit; there are other factors that break in on it. Most decisive of these is brain function, which in some way regulates the reflex.

Merleau-Ponty's immediate task is to explain this regulating function of the brain. More specifically, he wants to attack the empiricist's conception of the brain and show that facts require such a conception to be replaced by another one involving the notion of whole as form. The philosophical issues behind this task will appear as we proceed.

Let us examine, first, the precise character of the empiricist's conception. It can be expressed at two levels. At the formal level, the brain is conceived as constituting a functional whole only in the sense of a sum. Thus it is maintained that the brain functions as a collection of parts outside of parts, a collection of externally related parts. At the physiological level, the empiricist conceives the brain as a mosaic of points at which connections between afferent and efferent nerve pathways are determined.

It is especially important that this conception entails strict localization: any particular sector of behavior (such as vision) is regulated only by a certain definite part of the brain, namely, that part in which the relevant nerve pathways terminate. Various mental functions would be strictly localized.

Merleau-Ponty's argument, for all the complexity of detail, is relatively simple in its general outline. He presents data showing that there is no such strict localization of function. Since such localization is entailed by the empiricist's conception of the brain, this conception must be rejected. Furthermore, it must be replaced by a theory able to account for the peculiar pattern of localization and nonlocalization which the data reveal.

The most important source of data is Goldstein's investigations of the effects of cortical lesions. These investigations show, contrary to what empiricistic theory would lead us to expect, that a localized cortical lesion does not simply eliminate certain particular responses. What is lost is not a certain stock of movements but rather a certain level of action, not a particular circumscribed *sector* of behavior but a certain *level* of behavior. Merleau-Ponty quotes Goldstein: "Every time the affected person is obliged to depart from reality and enter the sphere of what is only 'possible' or only 'thought up,' he is doomed to fail" (SB 64, 69).

In other words, after a lesion there is a global disintegration. All the responses remain, but all of them operate at a more rudimentary level. There is loss in all sectors of what Goldstein calls the "categorial attitude." According to Merleau-Ponty: "It is evident that here the malady does not directly concern the content of behavior but rather its structure" (SB 64, 70).

Merleau-Ponty sums up the result of these investigations in the first of three theses: "A lesion, even localized, can determine structural disorders which concern the whole of behavior, and analogous structural disorders can be provoked by lesions situated in different regions of the cortex" (SB 62, 66).

This thesis contains two conclusions. First, the fact that lesions cause *structural* disorders affecting the *whole* of behavior shows that what is disrupted is not simply a connection point, a switch which connects afferent nerves to efferent ones. Rather, what is disrupted is a general or global organizational function. Therefore, the point of injury is normally involved not only in the localized function the empiricist ascribes to it but also in a global function pertaining to behavior as a whole. Second, the fact that analogous structural disorders can be caused by injuries to various points in the cortex shows that this organizational function is not itself strictly localized; the cortex as a whole is involved in this function. Thus over and against whatever localized functions there are, we find a nonlocalized global function of organization. This does not mean, however, that there is no localization in brain functioning; in other words, it does not mean that functionally the brain is an undifferentiated whole.

The "relative rights" of localization are established in a second thesis: "Nevertheless, nerve functioning cannot be treated as a global process in which all the parts of the system would intervene with the same weight. The function is never indifferent to the substrate by which it is realized" (SB 69, 76).

This thesis says that there is a degree of localization. The evidence is the fact that in cases of brain injury the specific character of the disorder is not totally independent of the place where the lesion occurs. What is decisive is indeed the *structural* disorder, but "the location of lesions determines as it were the principal point of application of structural disorders" (SB 70, 76). That is to say, cortical lesions produce a more pronounced deficiency in vision in one patient, in language in another, or in still a different sector in another, depending on the region of the brain where the lesion occurs.

Thus Merleau-Ponty wants to maintain both a global functioning and a localized functioning. This is what he means when he says in the third thesis that "place in nerve substance has an equivocal signification" (SB 72, 79).

Merleau-Ponty sums up the relation between these two kinds of function: "The facts which force us to admit a spatialization of the cerebral regions do not eliminate the relation of these regions to the whole *with regard to functioning.* Authors are also in agreement in accepting that the regions are not specialized in the reception of certain contents but rather in the structuration of the contents. Everything happens as if the regions were not the seat of certain anatomical devices but the terrain for the exercise of an activity of organization, applied, it is true, to a certain type of material" (SB 70–71, 77–78).

In conclusion, the brain functions neither as a mere collection of parts nor as an undifferentiated whole. There is localization in the sense that various regions are specialized for the structuration of certain contents. But this structuration is inserted into the framework of the whole, the framework of a global structuration.

Merleau-Ponty finally determines that the most appropriate categories here are the Gestalt categories of figure and ground. Global function is the ground; localized functioning is a figure placed on that background and standing out from it.

* * *

The remainder of this section presents several sets of psychological data concerning perceptual and linguistic behavior in support and illustration of the theory.

In general, what Merleau-Ponty wants to show is how the structural pattern inherent in brain functioning as such is carried over into the regulatory action of the brain. That is, he wants to show how in this regulatory action it is the pattern expressed in such concepts as form or figure-ground that is fundamental.

More specifically, Merleau-Ponty wants to show how the value of any stimulus (and hence the associated reflex) is determined not simply by the local excitation but rather also through the insertion of the local excitation within a whole. Let us follow one example to understand what this "insertion within a whole" signifies.

Merleau-Ponty refers to the fact that a window illuminated by neutral daylight appears bluish in a room lighted by the yellow light of electricity. The walls of that room appear faded and whitish, rather than having the yellow tint we would expect due to the illumination with yellow light. What is important is the curious color shift that takes place. An objectively yellow light has assumed the function of ground or neutral light. And an objectively neutral light has taken on a color value such that the same difference is maintained between it and the new neutral light.

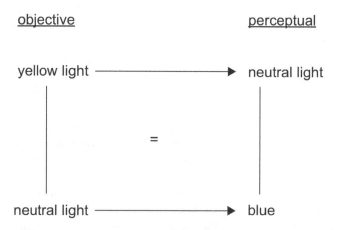

According to Merleau-Ponty: "It is a question of a sort of 'shift of level' by which the color playing the role of ground becomes neutral, while the color of the figure is modified in such a way that the difference between ground and figure remains invariable" (SB 81, 90). Merleau-Ponty sums up the significance of this example as follows: "The chromatic value which will be assigned in perception to some particular point of the visual field is not solely an effect combining local excitation and excitations simultaneously distributed on the retina. It also depends on the chromatic value assigned to the ground, and this value tends toward neutrality, no matter what the excitation received, in virtue of a law of equilibrium proper to the nervous system" (SB 82, 91).

The point is that the elaboration of each specific content is inserted in a global elaboration (structuration) of the perceptual field. A location in the brain specialized for some specific content does not function independently but rather determines this content in accord with a global organizational function. In other words, what we have on both sides (perceived, perceiver) is the Gestalt figure-ground structure.

On the basis of this exploration, Merleau-Ponty formulates three conclusions. They make explicit the philosophical issues.

(1) "It is not the real world which constitutes the perceived world" (SB 88, 97). The stimulus, as determined by and corresponding to the real world, the stimulus as it impinges on the organism, does not strictly determine the effect of the stimulus within the total act of perception. What I see is not simply determined by the visual stimuli impinging on my retinas. Rather, as the example shows, this stimulus is taken up into a global process of organization and transformation. Accordingly, through this global activity, the organism contributes to the constitution of the perceived world.

Therefore, the perceived world, as involving such a contribution, cannot be identified with the "real" world, the world considered independently of the organism.

(2) The essential demarcation is not between sensibility and intelligence (a chaos of impressions and a higher system that would organize them) but rather between different types or levels of organization.

This conclusion follows from the fact that the central nervous system does not simply organize into some pattern a mass of pregiven sensations; it does not simply take certain sense-contents and put them together. Instead, the very character of the stimulus is from the beginning determined by its insertion within global activity. As Chapter 1 already suggested, the organism contributes to the very constitution of the stimulus.

The philosophical import of this is obvious: if we associate the body with sensibility and consciousness with intelligence (synthesis), we can say that Merleau-Ponty has abolished the rigid separation between consciousness and body, and he has proposed to reinterpret this distinction in terms of various levels of organization.

(3) The appropriate categories for understanding perception are not those of physiology but those of psychology. More specifically, perception is explicable only through concepts taken from the perceived itself.

Here Merleau-Ponty is thinking primarily of the fact that the attempt he has made to carry through a physiological explanation has, in the end, led him to introduce the figure-ground concept, which is not a physiological concept but rather one borrowed from the perceived world: "The living physiology of the nervous system can only be understood by starting from phenomenal givens" (SB 88, 97).

There is another conclusion, one not stated explicitly but perhaps the most important. We can see it as a consequence of the first conclusion (the real world does not make the perceived world). The point is that the first conclusion recoils on the entire enterprise of understanding behavior, for behavior is presented perceptually, and it is on the basis of this presentation that the account proceeds.

This recoil has to be taken into consideration, for it alters the whole sense of the account of behavior: it becomes an account of the organism, not as something existing in itself, but as it presents itself to us. In other words, the objective character of the account is undercut—not by extrinsic criticism, but precisely through the account itself.

Here we see very clearly how Merleau-Ponty is performing a *phenomenological reduction*, how he is moving from a position which takes objects as simply existing independently of the subject, to a position which regards them in terms of their way of presenting themselves to the subject. And we see how he is doing this precisely by letting naturalism collapse under the weight of its own findings.

c.) The Structures of Behavior

This last major section of Chapter 2 follows the pattern of the whole chapter: a critique of the behaviorist concept of response at a higher level—this time at the level of learning.

In summary, Merleau-Ponty presents data showing that learning (adaptiveness) cannot be accounted for as the mere establishment of new connections between stimulus and response. On the contrary, a response (except in very extraordinary cases) is not a response to isolated stimuli but to a "situation for the organism." That is, the response takes place within a total context, one which is already "shot through" with internal connections and anticipations, a context the organism has already made *its* context.

Thus, learning—as the extension of the range of the organism's response—is not merely the establishing of a capacity to respond to larger numbers of stimuli. Instead, learning makes possible a response to a wider variety of situations.

But this is still insufficient; learning is not simply multiplying the number of particular situations to which the organism responds. Rather, learning has a *general character*. That is, learning involves acquiring the ability to respond not just to a new particular situation but to a whole range of situations which have the same formal structure though are materially different.

On this basis Merleau-Ponty classifies behavior in a new way, namely, in terms of the extent to which the structure emerges from material conditions.

The classification moves from syncretic forms (structure immersed in material conditions) through amovable forms (various degrees of emergence of structure) to symbolic forms (where structure can become so completely detached from material conditions that it alone becomes the real theme of activity).

d.) Conclusion

Here Merleau-Ponty concludes his long detour through behavioristic psychology. We need to see what this entire inquiry has established with respect to psychology.

It has revealed inadequacies in the foundations of classical behaviorism, has freed psychology from behaviorism. But it has not fully entitled the psychologist to ignore behaviorism. For, as Merleau-Ponty says, such critique is never finished. Behaviorism can always invent new mechanical models, and, furthermore, there is a "truth of naturalism."

We have called the whole critique a detour, which is to say that its ultimate intent is philosophical. So what does the detour achieve philosophically, and why was the detour necessary?

We have seen one consequence: the study of behavior must take into account the way behavior presents itself to us. That is, we cannot naively assume that behavior is something in-itself but must consider that it is available for inquiry only as it presents itself, only relative to the observer. It shows itself only as for-consciousness. We saw this in connection with the divergence between the perceived, phenomenal world and the real world.

But that is not the only consequence. Merleau-Ponty says that if it were, then the detour would not have been necessary. Invoking the *cogito* would have been sufficient. In other words, reflection would have sufficed to show that every object is an object for consciousness. Thus we could presumably have invoked the phenomenological reduction immediately. Merleau-Ponty explains: "But by following this short route we would have missed what is essential to the phenomenon, the paradox constitutive of it: behavior is not a thing, but neither is it an idea. It is not the envelope of a pure consciousness, and as the witness of behavior I am not a pure consciousness. It is precisely this which we wanted to express by saying that behavior is a form" (SB 127, 138).

There are two issues here, not clearly distinguished. We have referred already to the first: the question of the mode of being of behavior. Is behavior (as presented) thing or consciousness? Merleau-Ponty's account has shown that it is neither: not a thing, because behavior does not unfold as a series of physical, atomic (causal) events, each outside the other; and not consciousness, because behavior is not directed at the "true" objective world but at the world-for-the-organism. What is revealed in behavior is not a pure knowing of the world but rather a certain manner of treating the world, of being-in-the-world, of which a pure consciousness would be, in principle, incapable.

So behavior (neither thing nor consciousness) is a *form*, a Gestalt.

Yet Merleau-Ponty also says that behavior is not an idea and that as the witness of behavior I am not a pure consciousness. He means that behavior presents itself in *perceptual experience*, and its character (as presented) is determined by this fact. That is, behavior cannot be "translated" into an object of pure thought, an idea. Just as behavior cannot be dissolved into "real" parts, so it cannot be dissolved into an intelligible relational structure. It cannot be fully conceptualized.

That is what Merleau-Ponty showed in his criticism of the attempt at a physiological account. We can understand behavior only if we begin and remain with something familiar to us through perception alone, namely, the figure-ground structure. And that is why our preliminary definition of form was inadequate: it was a purely abstract, conceptual definition.

Most generally, this means that the critique of naturalism does not justify idealism. It does not simply replace behavior as thing with behavior as idea, something totally transparent to knowing consciousness, something which could be regarded as constituted by pure thought.

Instead, there is an *opaqueness* in behavior which prevents its being translated into an idea and assimilated to consciousness. This is the "truth of naturalism."

Merleau-Ponty sums up: "The structure of behavior as it presents itself to perceptual experience is neither thing nor consciousness; that is what renders it opaque to the mind" (SB 127, 138).

* * *

Chapter 3 is based entirely on these results and brings out the tension between a shift to the transcendental standpoint (every object as for-consciousness) and the retention of the truth of naturalism (residual opaqueness). In different terms, the third chapter brings to focus the tension between the fact that every object is for consciousness and the fact that consciousness is itself rooted in the vital (behavioral) and physical order. We see this rootedness already in the inability of thought to cut itself loose from perception.

In other words, Chapter 3 poses the problem of a transcendental consciousness which at the same time is rooted in a pre-conscious dimension, a consciousness which is transcendental without being absolute. It is from this problem that Merleau-Ponty's concept of phenomenology will arise.

D. Chapter 3 of *The Structure of Behavior*: The Physical Order, the Vital Order, the Human Order

IN THE FIRST two chapters, Merleau-Ponty has shown that behavior cannot be decomposed by causal analysis into physical elements. That means a distinction must be made between the field of behavior and the physical field—in the sense that the kind of structuration characteristic of behavior is not derivable from the kind of structuration we find in physical things.

Now Merleau-Ponty adds a third field, the mental field. Thus we have three orders: matter, life, mind; or physical order, vital order, human order. Merleau-Ponty's task is to examine these orders as they present themselves and to show how each order involves a distinctive kind of structure, its own peculiar *form*. In other words, he extends the category of form beyond behavior and applies it to all three orders, while yet showing that form is unique in each case. In this way he wants to account for both the autonomy of each level as well as the integration (coherence) of the three.

It is especially important to recognize that Merleau-Ponty interrogates these orders *as* they present themselves, as they announce both themselves and their differences to us. Thus what he finds in each case is a level of structure (form or Gestalt) not an order of being, not a type of substance (such as man versus animal).

Furthermore, Merleau-Ponty shows that if these orders are so regarded, then it is possible to avoid the classical antinomy between materialism and vitalism. As long as the orders are regarded as orders of substances, it is impossible to preserve both the autonomy and integration of the three levels.

The autonomy of the vital and mental could be preserved in terms of the opposition of substance to substance, which is that of mind to matter (Descartes) or *élan vital* to matter (Bergson). But in such a case, the integration (interaction) remains unintelligible, "magical."

Thus vitalism or mentalism tends to generate the opposite, materialism. Since the physical encompasses everything, the other two orders become reduced to it. And then integration is preserved but only by sacrificing the autonomy of the vital and mental.

Merleau-Ponty's point is that this antinomy arises only because we overlook the way these orders present themselves, and we conceive them instead as orders of being. It is not as orders of being but as types of structure that they announce themselves.

a.) Physical Structures

Merleau-Ponty considers the three orders in turn. In each case his immediate problem is to describe the type of structure involved in relation to its way of presenting itself.

I want to consider in detail only what is essential so as to follow the more fundamental development under way here, namely, the emergence of the problem and conception of a phenomenology of perception. Discussion of physical structure is not in this respect absolutely essential, though it is essential for the more immediate task of accounting for the autonomy and integration of the three levels.

I will begin by noting and summarizing three observations as regards physical forms:

(1) There are certain structural wholes (forms, Gestalten) in the physical order. What distinguishes these wholes is that each part is codetermined by all the others in such a way as to maintain equilibrium and resist deformation. When an external force comes to bear on the system, there is an internal redistribution of forces, and that preserves the character of the whole.

Yet beyond a certain threshold, there is qualitative change in the whole itself. Hence, there is a possibility of discontinuity, development by leaps or crises.

(2) Such structural wholes are presupposed by scientific laws. Laws are always related to such a whole and have a meaning only within a certain whole. For example, the laws of falling bodies have meaning only within the field of relatively stable forces in the neighborhood of the surface of the earth. If this field changes, the laws would change.

(3) Such wholes are not first discovered by scientific thought but are presupposed. They must be given prior to scientific thought. That is, they are originally given in perceptual experience.

What we in effect have as regards these observations is a more technical presentation (from within science itself) of what will be explicitly affirmed in the *Phenomenology of Perception*: science is a mere secondary expression of the world as directly (perceptually) experienced.

Let us look in a more detailed way at this development. The argument here is very complex. I will try to sketch its main lines in three steps:

(1) Such structural wholes are involved in all knowledge of physical nature, as was noted. But the converse holds as well: such structural wholes also presuppose scientific laws.

From the scientific perspective, such wholes are totalities of relations, and these relations are first established by scientific laws. It is such wholes which the laws try to express, indeed imperfectly. So these wholes are not starting points; instead, as conceptual, "thought wholes," they are the goal, the ideal toward which scientific thought moves.

(2) Accordingly, the relation between laws and structure is circular—even dialectical. Law presupposes structure, but it is precisely through the formulation of laws that structure, as object of thought, is constituted.

(3) This circularity is precisely what points back to the involvement, in scientific thought, of something prior to both law and structure. If scientific thought is ever to get under way—if it is to be able to set about determining laws, which, in turn, allow the constitution of the physical wholes—then the wholes must be pregiven, prior to scientific thought, so that laws can be formulated with respect to them. Furthermore, as the increasing use of perceptual models in physics clearly indicates, it is precisely in perception that these wholes are pregiven.

Therefore, at the root of the scientific *thought* of the objective world, we find the more primordial duality: perception—phenomena.

* * *

Let us examine the stage the inquiry has now reached. Throughout the first two chapters Merleau-Ponty's concern was to work out—primarily through empirical data—the distinction between the physical level and the behavioral level. Then at the beginning of Chapter 3 he proposes a tripartite stratification: physical order, vital order, human order. His immediate problem then is to distinguish each level by describing its characteristic structure and to show how at each level there is a reference back to consciousness, specifically to perceptual consciousness.

We sketched the way he carries this out for the physical order. Now we need to see how he achieves the same goal at the other levels. But some general comments, having to do with the difference between "structure" and "thing," are needed first. This difference is crucial because Merleau-Ponty is proposing to substitute a philosophy of structure for a philosophy of substances or things.

Structure is a complex or totality of relatedness, taking "relatedness" in the broadest sense. Relatedness, relations, can then be distinguished from the things that happen to be so related. For example, two numbers can be related by equality: $x = y$.

But the distinction strikes deeper than that. A thing is *en-soi*; it is conceived independently of the subject; it has attached to it the "thesis of the natural standpoint." But structure is not something in-itself; it is always "for consciousness";

it contains by its very nature a reference back to consciousness. It is precisely this "reference back" that Merleau-Ponty wants to demonstrate and explicate in this third chapter, and it has important consequences for understanding the overall character of *The Structure of Behavior*.

In developing a philosophy which articulates the world in terms of structure rather than being (in carrying out the shift from an in-itself to a for-consciousness), Merleau-Ponty has left behind the critique of psychology and entered into *phenomenology*. The task he undertakes in this chapter—regarded in its basic meaning—is nothing less than the performing of the *phenomenological reduction*, the suspending of the thesis of the natural attitude.

What is especially distinctive about the way Merleau-Ponty is here carrying out the phenomenological reduction, as compared with Husserl, is the way he shows the reduction to be motivated. Husserl, as already noted, paid a great deal of attention to this problem: how, living in the natural attitude, am I led—motivated—to suspend the thesis definitive of this attitude and carry out the reduction. What Merleau-Ponty has tried to show—and this is what is philosophically so important about much of *The Structure of Behavior*—is precisely how within the natural attitude, specifically through a critique of a science bound to the natural attitude, the phenomenological reduction is motivated, namely, by the natural attitude cracking under its own weight.

b.) Vital Structures

The critique of behaviorism allowed a distinction between the vital and physical orders. This distinction was drawn primarily by pointing to the necessity of employing the category of form for the vital order. But now we have seen that there is also form at the physical level. So the distinction has to be restated to show how form (structure) differs in the two orders. Merleau-Ponty reviews the description of physical structure and then says: "We speak of vital structures, on the contrary, when equilibrium is obtained, not with respect to real and present conditions, but with respect to conditions which are only virtual and which the system itself brings into existence—when the structure, instead of procuring a release from the forces with which it is penetrated through the pressure of external ones, executes a work beyond its own proper limits and constitutes a proper milieu for itself" (SB 145–46, 157).

Merleau-Ponty is speaking here of equilibrium and suggesting that what distinguishes the vital order is the character of the equilibrium, the preferred states, which the whole tends to preserve. More specifically, what distinguishes the vital order is the way these preferred states are determined. According to Merleau-Ponty: "Most of the time, preferred behavior is the simplest and most economical behavior *with respect to the task in which the organism finds itself engaged*" (SB 147, 159). That is, the preferred states are determined not simply in terms of the pressure and configuration of forces but rather in terms of tasks, in terms of the organism's engagement in certain kinds of tasks within a certain kind of milieu. Thus the preferred states are determined with respect to a certain way of being in the world.

Let us try to express it more precisely. The distinctive character of vital structure is this: any element (such as a stimulus) in the scope of the structure is determined by the *significance* it has for the organism. Merleau-Ponty says: "The reactions evoked by a stimulus depend on the significance it has for the organism" (SB 147, 159).

But how does such significance arise? How can a stimulus be significant? It can be so only in relation to a total (global) way of being toward or in the world. Yet, in turn, such a way of being in the world points back to a fundamental dialectical engagement between organism and world.

In simple terms, the world makes certain demands, calls for certain tasks. The organism, in turn, delineates its milieu with regard to these tasks. On the other hand, the world was able to call for certain tasks in the first place only insofar as it was already taken up and delimited by the organism. What we have here is a circular, dialectic process: "This signifies that the organism itself measures the action of things on it and delimits its milieu by a circular process without analogue in the physical world. The relations of the organic individual and its milieu are thus truly dialectical relations, and this dialectic brings about the appearance of new relations which cannot be compared with those of a physical system and its surroundings" (SB 148, 161).

Accordingly, vital structure (as dialectical) has no analogy in the physical order and cannot be accounted for in physical terms. But this does not mean that over and above a level of physical processes we must introduce another existing force, a vital force which would somehow fill the gap left in a purely physical explanation of an organism. Instead, "the idea of signification permits conserving the category of life without the hypothesis of a vital force" (SB 155, 168). That is to say, what we find in the organism that physical description cannot account for is not some "missing link" in a chain of causality. Rather, it is a unity of meaning, a signification: "Vital acts *have* a meaning" (SB 159, 172).

Yet meaning is not a thing to be added to other things. On the contrary, it can reveal itself only to a subject, to consciousness. Merleau-Ponty says of the organism: "it is a whole which is significant for a consciousness which knows it; it is not a thing which rests in itself" (SB 159, 172). Again he says: "The object of biology is unthinkable without the unities of signification which a consciousness finds and sees unfolding in it. . . . What we have designated under the name of life was already the consciousness of life" (SB 161–62, 175). And this consciousness is fundamentally a perceptual consciousness: the organism "is given in perception with the original characteristics we have described" (SB 159, 172).

c.) The Human Order

The structure of the argument in this section can be expressed in three steps:

(1) Preliminary answer to the question of the new factor, the new dialectic, that appears when we pass from the vital order to the human order.

(2) Discussion of consciousness as lived and definition of consciousness as intentionality, in response to the question of how consciousness must be understood in order to allow for the new dialectic.

(3) Establishing of the fundamental character of human dialectic as continual movement of transcendence.

Let us now look at these steps in detail.

(1) What do we find in the human order that is new, that distinguishes it from the vital order? Initially, at least, this new factor would seem to lie in the fact that man creates a new milieu for himself (rather than simply delimiting a milieu). This he does through *work* (in its Hegelian sense). Through work, man places between himself and the world a new world of use-objects and cultural objects.

As Hegel and Marx recognized, work is thoroughly dialectical: through work man transforms his situation, and in turn, by transforming his situation, man transforms his own behavior, which is always behavior in a situation. Thus the terms of the new dialectic which comes forth with the human order are: perceived situation—work.

At this point, Merleau-Ponty is not so much interested in exploring that dialectic itself. Rather, he wants to discover what the dialectic entails for our understanding of human consciousness and action. More specifically, he raises this question: how must work (action) and especially consciousness be conceived so that this dialectic between them is possible?

(2) Consciousness as lived, as intentionality.

Traditionally, consciousness and action have both been understood in a way which made any "internal communication" between them incomprehensible. Consciousness is conceived as the possession of certain thought-contents; action is conceived as a series of events external to one another. Under these terms, it is difficult to see how consciousness makes any contact with existing things, much less with action.

Merleau-Ponty elaborates the problem in reference to a more or less Kantian conception of consciousness, according to which there is a certain apriori form originating in consciousness and distinguishable from the empirical (aposteriori) contents to which it is applied and which it organizes.

What disturbs Merleau-Ponty in this conception is the fact that all specifications of experience are based on aposteriori contents: the difference between consciousness of a material thing, consciousness of a use-object, and consciousness of another person is strictly a result of the difference between the respective sensory contents. This would entail that, for example, in the perception of another person, I "get at" the other person only through the *interpretation* of a mass of sense-data. I reconstruct the person from sense contents rather than recognizing the person immediately.

In opposition, Merleau-Ponty maintains that perception of the other person is *originary*. That is to say, it is not as though I first have a mass of sense-data which I subsequently interpret as representing another person, a mass of sensible signs through the interpretation of which I could then discover something human: a smile, for example, and the human meaning it embodies. Instead, I immediately grasp the expression in a human face, before I grasp any of its objective features. A common example would be the experience of knowing someone well without knowing the color of the person's eyes: "It follows from this that it is possible to perceive a smile, or even the sentiment in this smile, without the colors and lines (which, as is said, 'compose' the face) being present to consciousness or given in an unconsciousness. . . . The human signification is given before the alleged sensible signs" (SB 166–67, 180–81).

In the language of the *Phenomenology of Perception*: I do not have to reconstruct the other person from something else. The other person is always already there. In Scheler's terminology this is an instance of a *material apriori*, and if we follow up this concept we can see how it leads to a new conception of consciousness.

It is clear that consciousness cannot be defined as a universal function of the organization of sensory contents. Such a conception would permit only a *formal apriori*. That is, it would relegate all material (nonformal) specification to the variety of contents. Instead, Merleau-Ponty maintains that material specifications (regions, in Husserl's sense) are *originary*, are always already sketched out in the lived world: I perceive something human; I do not reconstruct, *represent* it from something else which I perceive.

The same is true of use-objects (Heidegger): I grasp a tool as a tool; I do not first perceive it as a thing with qualities and then add some further attribute or value to it.

But if such regions are always already "sketched out," this points in turn to the fact that consciousness is capable of many different types of acts, corresponding to the various regions. Thus consciousness is not merely the formal activity of representation. Rather, representation (knowing) is only one way consciousness may be related to an object. Therefore consciousness must be defined not as representation but as *intentionality*.

This brings us to a crucial distinction: representation, theoretical knowing, judgment is always (according to the tradition) more or less self-transparent. That is, self-consciousness, the "I think," as Kant puts it, must always be able to accompany my representations. In short, consciousness is self-consciousness.

But for Merleau-Ponty not all consciousness is representational. And, in turn, not all consciousness is permeated with the self-transparency of self-consciousness: "What we have said is sufficient to show that the possession of a representation or the exercise of a judgment is not coextensive with the life of consciousness. Instead, consciousness is a network of significative intentions, sometimes clear to themselves and sometimes, on the contrary, lived rather than known" (SB 173, 187). It is on the level of "lived consciousness" that "internal communication" between consciousness and action becomes conceivable. Merleau-Ponty's example has to do with a player on a soccer field:

> Certain states of adult consciousness permit us to comprehend this distinction. For the player in action the soccer terrain is not an "object," that is, an ideal term which can give rise to an indefinite multiplicity of perspectival views and remain equivalent under its apparent transformations. It is pervaded with lines of force (the "sidelines" or the lines demarcating the "penalty area") and articulated in sectors (for example, the "holes" amid the defenders) which call for a certain mode of action and which initiate and bear the action as if the player were unaware of it. The terrain is not *given* to him, but present as the immanent term of his practical intentions; the player becomes one with it and feels the direction of the "goal," for example, just as immediately as the vertical and horizontal planes of his own body. It would not be sufficient to say that consciousness *inhabits* this milieu. At the moment, consciousness is nothing other than the dialectic of milieu and action. Each maneuver undertaken by the player modifies the aspect of the terrain and establishes in it new lines of force in which the action in turn unfolds and is carried out, again altering the phenomenal field. (SB 168–69, 182–83)

We can anticipate the implications of this for political action and can say at least that such action is not a matter of the theoretical formulation of ends which praxis would simply apply. Instead, action is tied to ("communicates with") what is lived in the situation. The abrupt transition in Merleau-Ponty's own career from thought to action is thus perhaps not as abrupt as it appears.

(3) Human dialectic as movement of transcendence. We have seen that consciousness is such that it can intend its objects in various ways. The inquiry has suggested, however, that the fundamental distinction here is between consciousness as knowing and consciousness as lived. In turn, the question thereby raised concerns the relation (transition) between these.

Merleau-Ponty proceeds to trace out this transition (lived → knowing). It is in effect the capacity for this movement which Merleau-Ponty identifies as the essence of man, as that which genuinely distinguishes the human order. How so?

We have seen that with the transition to the human order, we discover the phenomenon of work, the capacity to create "a second nature . . . beyond biological nature" (SB 175, 189). Man inserts use-objects between himself and nature. But this creating of a second nature is *not* what defines man. One could, after all, maintain that when Köhler's chimps take a stick and use it as a tool, they too are placing a use-object between themselves and nature.

What is it then that distinguishes man? Merleau-Ponty describes it as "the capacity of going beyond created structures in order to create others" (SB 175, 189). The essential point is that man does not lose himself in the new nature he creates; he remains capable of multiple perspectives. He does not remain immersed in the lived; the lived "does not exhaust the human dialectic" (SB 175, 189). For example, the stick which has become a tool is for the chimp now simply a tool. For man, it is a stick-become-tool and can become still something else.

Thus the animal remains imprisoned in concrete situations; but man can orient himself to the mediate, the virtual, the possible: man is capable of the "categorial attitude" (SB 176, 190). That means man is able to relate himself to things in a way that is not bound to his concrete perceptual viewpoint but which is rather a movement toward the *transcendence* of all points of view. This is the movement involved in the origination of theoretical consciousness.

So Merleau-Ponty quotes Scheler: "Man is a being who has the power of elevating to the status of objects the centers of resistance and actions of his milieu . . . among which animals live entranced" (SB 176, 191).

d.) Conclusion

The problem of the three orders was posed as that of retaining both the autonomy of each level and the integration of all or, as Merleau-Ponty puts it, of liberating the higher from the lower and yet founding the higher on the lower.

It could be said that each order is related to the next higher one as part to whole. Each order initiates a new, more comprehensive kind of unity in which the lower orders are taken up and transformed.

Recall how the vital order—in contrast to the physical—is not a self-enclosed unity merely resisting external forces but rather opens up onto a situation and is a unity involving both organism and situation. Likewise, the human order is no mere dialectic of organism and situation but rather subsumes this dialectic into a more comprehensive dialectic of man and world.

Accordingly, Merleau-Ponty says: "The advent of higher orders, to the extent that they are accomplished, eliminates the autonomy of the lower orders and gives a new signification to the steps which constitute them" (SB 180, 195).

Nevertheless, the higher orders remain founded on the lower orders inasmuch as the higher are structures which integrate the lower and are not substances superimposed on them: "One does not act with mind alone. . . . Because it is not a new sort of being but a new form of unity, mind cannot stand by itself" (SB 181, 196).

E. Chapter 4 of *The Structure of Behavior*: The Relations of the Soul and the Body and the Problem of Perceptual Consciousness

a.) Situated Consciousness

Through his critique of naturalism, Merleau-Ponty brought the inquiry to the level of the transcendental standpoint. At the same time, he suggested that such a detour was necessary in order to carry over into this standpoint a certain truth of naturalism. The problem is how this truth of naturalism can be made to accord with the transcendental perspective.

The inquiry in Chapter 3 was pursued from such a perspective, yet in a way that brought out the tension between the transcendental perspective and the truth of naturalism. Chapter 4 is then an explicit statement of the full problematic generated by this tension. It is exactly this problematic which defines Merleau-Ponty's "phenomenological standpoint," and it is the problematic which the *Phenomenology of Perception* will seek to explore (cf. the "Prospectus").

Let us consider the transcendental standpoint, the one from which everything is for-consciousness. The crucial question that thereby arises can be formulated in two ways.

First, if everything is for-consciousness, then does this apply also to consciousness itself? Is consciousness something for consciousness? Is consciousness merely for-itself? Is consciousness simply self-consciousness? Is consciousness totally transparent to itself? Or, rather, is there perhaps some inherent opaqueness at the heart of consciousness, an unclarity that cannot be dissipated?

Second, the same question can be formulated in terms of the outcome of Chapter 3. We were given two views of consciousness. On the one hand, everything is for-consciousness. That is to say, consciousness is presupposed by each level as that to which it announces its distinctive form, and therefore consciousness is the "universal milieu." But consciousness also appeared as one of the three orders and in this connection was seen to be rooted in the lower levels. So how are these two views of consciousness to be brought together? "What then is the relation between consciousness as universal milieu and consciousness as rooted in the subordinated dialectics?" (SB 184, 189).

Merleau-Ponty wants to preserve both views of consciousness. Clearly this requires that the rootedness of consciousness be understood in a new way, not as a rootedness in something merely external (in the body as a material thing).

Merleau-Ponty tries to understand this rootedness in terms of a "constitutive history": consciousness arises only out of such a history, and accordingly consciousness is not something "guaranteed" but rather is an accomplishment with its origins (history) in the lower, already achieved, already constituted levels.

Now we can reformulate the question with which we began: Can consciousness transform its own history into something for-itself? In other words, can consciousness transform the history which constitutes it into something it itself constitutes? Can consciousness retrieve its origins and render them totally transparent?

If consciousness could do so, it would mean that consciousness could totally free itself from its history and hence could avoid retaining in itself any of the opaqueness characteristic of the lower stages. The dialectic of consciousness would simply be its development into self-consciousness. In terms we used earlier, the dialectic would be one in which the rational totally absorbs the pre-rational and eliminates its character as pre-rational.

Under what conditions would that be possible? Only if the constitutive history of consciousness, the lower levels on which it appears to depend, have a certain character such that their positive content is reducible to something for-consciousness. They must be distinguished from the level of consciousness only negatively, privatively, as levels of confused consciousness.

Now we can see Merleau-Ponty's problem. He refuses to grant consciousness complete autonomy with respect to its history. However much consciousness may be a universal milieu, it still remains *essentially* rooted in the lower levels: it is not absolute consciousness (pure self-consciousness) but rather is *situated consciousness*. In other words, the lower levels cannot simply be carried over into consciousness without residue.

Therefore, Merleau-Ponty's task is to interrogate the lower levels and demonstrate their *originality*: there is something characteristic of them making them irreducible to the relation of knowing consciousness to its object. Specifically, Merleau-Ponty first must identify these lower levels which form the constitutive history. These levels cannot simply be equated with the physical and vital orders of Chapter 3, for those have a different significance when they become constituents of the human order versus the character they have when alone. His second task is to demonstrate the irreducibility of the lower levels.

b.) Transcendental Philosophy

Merleau-Ponty carries out the first of these two tasks by tracing the emergence of the transcendental attitude in modern philosophy since Descartes.

In general, Merleau-Ponty finds this attitude objectionable because it has excluded the original, irreducible character of the lower levels from which consciousness emerges.

What specifically is it that the traditional transcendental attitude excludes? What are these lower levels which get reduced to the level of consciousness?

Of course, Merleau-Ponty is in agreement with transcendental philosophy in one respect: such philosophy does not situate itself in a ready-made world. It does not, like realism, separate soul, body, and object as three things and then try to account for experience in terms of the causal action of the object on the body or of the body on the soul.

How then does transcendental philosophy proceed? As we see with the Cartesian *cogito* and the Kantian "Copernican Revolution," transcendental philosophy situates itself *within* experience. In place of a realistic account, it substitutes a reflection upon, a *thinking* directed upon, experience and the things experienced. A *thinking* about the perceived, however, can reveal only the intelligible structure (meaning, essence) of the object. In particular, it cannot account for the presence of the object, for the "existential index" accompanying it.

Merleau-Ponty points to this problem as it arises in the Kantian tradition, where experience involves, in addition to the conscious apprehension of meaning (intelligible structure) also the presence of a "given"—which presumably would account for this existential index. But the Kantian tradition finds it impossible to say what this given is. If we try to isolate the perceived content, we find that at every level there is already an activity of consciousness involved. Empirical content becomes a mere "borderline notion," a limit-concept.

Therefore the existential index is not really taken into account. In the end, everything is simply *for* thinking consciousness. And that applies even to the body: it is only an object-for-consciousness.

* * *

The problematic sketched in Chapter 4 is essentially the problematic of the *Phenomenology of Perception*. Hence it is important to have it well in our grasp. At the same time, this problematic is very difficult to understand because it takes for granted a familiarity with the whole tradition of transcendental philosophy and especially with phenomenology.

So before we proceed to complete our sketch of the problematic, I want to go back and trace out more systematically and in the simplest possible terms some of basic ideas and issues of transcendental philosophy, ones with which Merleau-Ponty more or less assumes familiarity. Then we will be able to see much better that aspect of his problematic we have just sketched, and we will be in a better position for completing the sketch and then moving into the *Phenomenology of Perception*. Many of these issues of transcendental philosophy will be taken up explicitly in that book, so it will help to have them well in mind in advance.

I want to begin at the simplest level and gradually build up the problematic in a series of six steps:

(1) Consider first of all the contrast between intellectual consciousness and perceptual consciousness. Intellectual consciousness aims at an idea; perceptual consciousness aims at a perceptual object. We can best see the contrast if we consider the character of the object to which each type of consciousness is directed.

The object of intellectual consciousness (an idea) is simply a product of the activity of consciousness. We do not encounter ideas; instead, we form them (by abstraction). Of course, it may be that this production is not a creation ex nihilo; it may be that a certain given material is necessary in order for consciousness to form ideas. Nevertheless, ideas as such originate from the activity of thought: they are constituted by thought.

The perceptual object, on the other hand, is encountered. That is to say, it does not present itself as merely constituted, merely formed by some activity on my part. It presents itself as existing independently of my activity of perceiving it and accordingly possesses an "existential index." It presents itself as having already been there before I turned to it in an act of perception.

So we arrive at this contrast between consciousness of an ideal object and consciousness of a real object.

(2) Now we introduce a third type of consciousness: reflective consciousness. Considered simply as an activity, reflection does not seem to differ from intellectual consciousness. In both cases, the activity involved is that of thought; we speak of reflection as reflective *thought*. Therefore if we abstract from its relation to its object, reflective consciousness is the same as intellectual consciousness.

But the object of reflective consciousness (what it intends) is quite different from that of intellectual consciousness. Reflection involves consciousness turning back on itself, taking itself as an object. More specifically, reflective consciousness has as its object the other types of consciousness; it is consciousness of consciousness.

Note that in our first step, where we described the types of consciousness, we—as doing the description—were already operating at the level of reflection.

(3) Now we need to bring into our account the fact that consciousness is intentionality, is always consciousness of. What does that mean? It does not simply mean that consciousness is always directed toward an object rather than,

for example, toward impressions or representations. Instead, it also means that the character of a conscious act cannot be described independently of the object intended in that act. Accordingly, consciousness cannot be described as some general activity (unification) such that it would be the same in every case regardless of the object intended. It is not as though all conscious activity is identically the same kind of activity simply related to different objects (or applied to different material).

Instead, the kind of object intended determines the kind of conscious activity involved. (Recall how Merleau-Ponty distinguishes between consciousness of another person and consciousness of a material object.) So it is impossible to separate consciousness from its object, to interrogate consciousness independently of what it intends.

(4) The intentional character of consciousness has two important consequences. First, it allows for the possibility of a radical distinction between different types of consciousness—specifically between perceptual consciousness and intellectual consciousness. These no longer need to be regarded as the same kind of activity, simply directed to different types of objects. Rather, the fact that they intend very different kinds of objects requires that they too be quite different. Note that when we drew the distinction between intellectual consciousness and perceptual consciousness we did so primarily in terms of the difference between their objects.

A second consequence with respect to the character of reflective consciousness is that reflection (consciousness of consciousness) cannot have as its object *merely* our conscious activity. Instead, since this conscious activity is inseparable from what it intends, reflection must encompass both the intentional activity and what it intends. That is, the object of reflective thought is not simply some intentional activity, not simply consciousness independent of its intended object, but rather is both the intentional activity and the intentional object in their interrelation. In Husserl's terms, a reflective investigation must be a noetic-noematic one.

So this schema results:

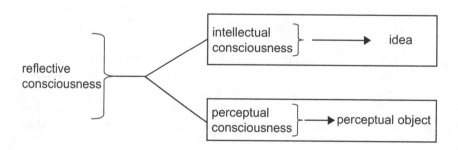

(5) Now we need to consider the structure of reflection. Suppose that reflection is executed at the level of intellectual consciousness.

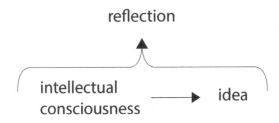

What is the character of the object intended by such reflection, and how is it intended?

On the noematic side (with respect to an idea), what reflection discovers is that an idea is merely a product of thought. But how does it discover this? Precisely by *thinking the idea*, by reenacting the activity of thought which constitutes the idea. That means reflective thought reenacts the noetic side, the intellectual consciousness, which first constituted the idea.

It means in turn that in reflection at the intellectual level the activity of thought (already accomplished by the first-level consciousness) is made explicit by being reenacted.

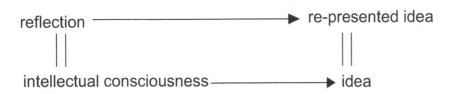

Finally, it means that reflection discovers that the object of intellectual consciousness is only a product of consciousness, that in knowing its object intellectual consciousness knows only itself. In other words, it is made explicit that at this level consciousness is simply self-consciousness.

(6) Consider now the case of reflection on the perceptual level.

Here we need to consider a hypothetical situation in order to see Merleau-Ponty's problem. Suppose reflective thought were able to think the perceptual object, build up the perceptual object, re-present it. That is, suppose reflection were able to exhibit the perceptual object as simply a product of the activity of

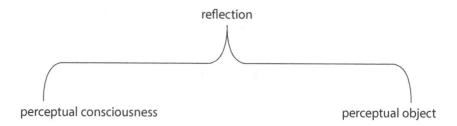

reflection

perceptual consciousness

perceptual object

thought, as capable of being reduced *without any residue* into a structure constituted by thought.

The consequence would be, first, that the perceptual object—just like an idea—is simply constituted by consciousness. Hence we are in the position of idealism.

Second, perceptual consciousness, in which the perceptual object is originally constituted, would not be essentially different from the reflective thought which reenacts its constitutive activity. If perceptual consciousness were essentially different, reflective thought could not reenact it adequately so as to represent the perceptual object.

Third, perceptual consciousness, just like intellectual consciousness, is then essentially self-consciousness. In being conscious of its object, it is conscious only of the product of its own activity: it is conscious only of itself. Hence in the end all consciousness is essentially self-consciousness.

The fourth consequence is that perceptual consciousness would be distinguished only by the fact that it is *implicit* self-consciousness. Reflection simply makes explicit what consciousness always already is implicitly, namely, self-consciousness.

* * *

Against this background we can better understand the issues we just discussed. I will make four points:

(1) What Merleau-Ponty calls into question is this raising of perceptual consciousness to the level of self-consciousness. That is, he wants to insist that perceptual consciousness is not merely implicit self-consciousness.

That means the object of perceptual consciousness cannot be exhibited (in reflective thought) as merely the product of thought. In other words, perception is not just confused thought, a thought which in being conscious of its object is implicitly conscious only of itself.

(2) To insist, however, that the perceptual object is not reducible to something constituted by thought does not mean to fall back into naturalism and regard the object as existing in itself.

Nor is it a matter of regarding the perceptual object as some kind of joint product "co-constituted" by consciousness and by something-in-itself. That would be only a half-hearted realism.

Instead, Merleau-Ponty situates himself within experience itself and does not pretend to be able to occupy some position above and beyond experience. That means he proceeds reflectively, proceeds by reflection on experience and on the objects of experience *as* they present themselves in experience. In that respect, Merleau-Ponty is aligned with transcendental philosophy, which insists on regarding every object as for-consciousness or, in other words, with respect to the way the object shows itself to consciousness.

(3) So, if it is to be shown that the perceptual object is not reducible to an object of thought—that perceptual experience is in this sense *original*—then this must be shown, not through positing some thing-in-itself behind the perceptual object, but rather through reflection itself. It is precisely such a reflective interrogation, one which brings to light the originality of perceptual experience, which constitutes a phenomenology of perception.

(4) The last chapter of *The Structure of Behavior* indicates what is to be uncovered by the reflective investigations of the *Phenomenology of Perception*.

Merleau-Ponty refers to the notion of a constitutive history *and* to the fact that perceptual consciousness has its rootedness in such a history. He wants to say that perceptual experience presupposes an already constituted basis which is granted by a constitutive history. Furthermore, this basis cannot be reduced to a product of thought, hence cannot be reduced to something constituted by consciousness.

In other words, consciousness cannot transform the history which constitutes it into a history which it constitutes. Moreover, since this basis cannot be dissolved into a product of thought and since it is precisely the basis for perceptual experience, the result is that perceptual experience as a whole is *original*, is not just implicit self-consciousness.

c.) The Irreducibility of Perceptual Experience

In Chapter 4 of *The Structure of Behavior*, Merleau-Ponty takes some initial steps toward interrogating the irreducible dimension of perceptual experience and hence toward indicating the principal lines his interrogation will follow in the *Phenomenology of Perception*. We need to consider three steps:

The first relates the body to the notion of a constitutive history.
The second provides a first indication as to what renders perceptual experience irreducible.
The third step deals with the relation of the body to perception.

(1) The body.

Merleau-Ponty's critique of naturalism has shown that the body cannot be regarded as some kind of material apparatus in which the soul resides, like a pilot in a ship. Instead, Merleau-Ponty proposes to understand the body in terms of the notion of a constitutive history. Specifically, the body comprises the way the constitutive history is present to consciousness. Merleau-Ponty says regarding the relation of the soul to the body that it is "a presence to consciousness of its proper history and of the dialectical stage it has traversed" (SB 208, 225).

More comprehensively, Merleau-Ponty describes the relation this way:

> The notions of soul and body must be relativized: there is the body as mass of chemical components in interaction, the body as dialectic of living being and its biological milieu, and the body as dialectic of social subject and its group; even all our habits are an impalpable body for the ego of each moment. Each of these degrees is soul with respect to the preceding one, body with respect to the following one. The body in general is an ensemble of paths already traced, of powers already constituted; the body is the acquired dialectical soil upon which a higher "formation" is accomplished, and the soul is the meaning which is then established. (SB 210, 227)

So the body is the presence of the past, the past not just as something remembered but as providing an effective basis for the present. In the body the past is present as something accomplished, as an "acquired dialectical soil," an "already constituted power."

In the *Phenomenology of Perception*, this basis will prove to be such that it disallows transformation into a product of thought. It is a way of being that is rooted in a history, whereby it is impossible for consciousness to transform the history which constitutes it into a history it constitutes.

The body is the way the mind has its past borne in its present depths. The relation of the problem of the body to the problem of temporality is evident.

(2) Merleau-Ponty provides a first indication of what renders perceptual consciousness irreducible to intellectual consciousness, what saves perception from being merely confused thought. He returns to naive perceptual experience as it is lived prior to the complications philosophical theory introduces.

Reflection on this experience reveals that access to an object is always an access by way of *profiles*: the perceptual object always presents itself only through profiles. I see things only from a certain direction, from a certain standpoint. But this fact does not mean perception yields only aspects, only profiles. Instead, I grasp the thing through its profiles, without, of course, ever exhausting all possible profiles: "I grasp *in* a perspectival aspect, which I know is only one of its possible aspects, the thing itself which transcends that aspect" (SB 187, 202).

It is especially significant that the perceptual object is never completely revealed. It is precisely the inexhaustibility of this object that defines, as Husserl says, its transcendence (or, as Merleau-Ponty says, its character as something real, something existing) and gives it its "existential index": "From the beginning, the perspectival character of knowledge is known as such and is not something to which we are subjected. Far from introducing a coefficient of subjectivity into perception, it on the contrary provides perception with the assurance of communicating with a world richer than what we know of it, that is, of communicating with a real world" (SB 186, 201).

What is crucial for Merleau-Ponty's argument is the difference between the perceptual object with its profile-structure and an object of intellectual consciousness (idea or signification): "This sensible mass in which I live when I stare at a sector of the field without trying to recognize it, the 'this' which my consciousness wordlessly intends, is not a signification or an idea, although subsequently it can serve as a basis for acts of logical explicitation and verbal expression" (SB 211, 228).

This is a difficult contrast to thematize, and Merleau-Ponty does not develop it in detail here. He merely illustrates it as the contrast between a cube as geometrical idea (six equal sides) and the cube as perceived (three unequal sides).

The general point is clear: what distinguishes perception and makes it irreducible to thought is its profile-structure. On the other hand—complicating the issue—this does not mean there is no perspectivism in ideas. But Merleau-Ponty does not discuss the perspectivism of ideas except to note that it is radically different from that of perceived things (for example, it does not provide the idea with an "existential index").

(3) Finally, Merleau-Ponty turns to the question of the relation of the body to perception. In general, as we saw, to have a body means to have an already constituted basis, to have a constitutive history present in such a way as to provide an acquired soil for one's acts.

What kind of basis does perception require? It requires that I occupy a standpoint, that I perceive from a standpoint, because to say that an object reveals itself through profiles is to say that it unfolds in relation to a standpoint from which it is viewed: "How could I receive an object 'in a certain direction' if I, the perceiving subject, were not in some way hidden in one of my phenomena, one which envelopes me since I cannot examine it from other viewpoints? Two points are necessary for determining a direction" (SB 214, 231).

Thus the body is the already constituted basis on which perception with its profile structure takes place: "To say that I have a body is simply another way of saying that my knowledge is an individual dialectic in which intersubjective objects appear, that these objects, when they are given to knowledge in the mode of actual existence, present themselves to it by successive aspects which cannot coexist; finally, it is a way of saying that one of them offers itself obstinately 'from the same side' and I cannot examine it from other viewpoints" (SB 213, 230).

This perhaps raises more questions than it answers. But it does serve to indicate the locus of the problem of the body, namely, as the problem of that constitutive history which provides the basis for perceptual experience.

*   *   *

The Structure of Behavior concludes by posing some questions with regard to the relation between "naturalized consciousness," that is, perceptual consciousness, and the "pure consciousness of self": "Can perceptual consciousness be thought without eliminating it as an original mode? Can its specificity be maintained without rendering unthinkable its relation to intellectual consciousness?" (SB 224, 241).

Here two problems are expressed. They are the difficult—perhaps the most difficult—problems the *Phenomenology of Perception* tries to work out. And there is reason to believe these problems were the primary ones provoking the further development of Merleau-Ponty's thought after the *Phenomenology of Perception*. Let us state them briefly.

(1) If we insist on the originality of perceptual consciousness, how are we to relate it to intellectual consciousness? The simple act of abstraction or judgment indicates how easily we do in fact move from perception to thought. How then is that transition to be accounted for? This is the *problem of the origin of truth.*

(2) Merleau-Ponty wants to show that perception is irreducible to thought. But this has to be shown by reflection, by reflective thought. Yet, if reflective thought is able to grasp the perceptual sphere, to penetrate it, to reveal it, to *think* the perceptual object, then this amounts to saying that perception *is* reducible to thought. And if reflection cannot penetrate perception, how can it establish anything about it? In general, how can it be established by thought that something is irreducible to thought? This we can call the *problem of reflection.*

II. PHENOMENOLOGY OF PERCEPTION

A. The Preface of the *Phenomenology of Perception*

Husserl famously summarized the basic intent of phenomenology in this expression: *zu den Sachen selbst*. We have seen something of what this return "to the things themselves" means for Merleau-Ponty: things are to be described rather than explained or analyzed.

That is to say, each thing is to be regarded *as* it presents itself, *as* it shows itself to consciousness, *as* it is for consciousness. This is a matter of returning to things the way they present themselves prior to being covered over by the concepts of philosophy, of science, and of common sense (recall the example of the cube).

Phenomenology is thus inherently transcendental: everything is regarded as it presents itself, as it is for consciousness. Here we need to obviate three common misconceptions:

(1) Husserl's dictum has sometimes been taken as a return to realism, to a conception of real things existing "out there," independently of consciousness.

But clearly this is not what is meant. In fact, the uncriticized belief in things existing in themselves (thesis of the natural standpoint) is to be suspended in favor of an interrogation which considers things as phenomena, as they present themselves. This suspension is the phenomenological reduction.

(2) At the other extreme, it has been maintained that phenomenology is inherently idealistic, that by suspending belief in the independent existence of things, phenomenology makes it impossible to grant that things are other than mere products of conscious activity.

But again this misses the point: the reduction does not deny independent existence to things but only suspends our naive belief in this existence so as to interrogate it. In other words, phenomenology tries to understand how it is that we attribute independent existence to things, how—on the basis of the way things present themselves—we come to regard them as existing in themselves. In Merleau-Ponty's terms, it is a question of how there can be an in-itself for-consciousness.

Thus phenomenology surpasses the alternatives of realism-idealism.

(3) Phenomenology requires that we situate ourselves in experience and attend to things as they present themselves. This has been taken to mean that phenomenology is a mere beholding in which we simply live through our engagement with things rather than thinking about that engagement.

But that is not so. Phenomenology, like all philosophy since Descartes, is reflective: phenomenology is not a matter of just living through our experience but of executing a reflection on experience and on things as experienced.

So Merleau-Ponty's phenomenology is a reflection on our originary experience in which things first show themselves, namely, perceptual experience. But Merleau-Ponty's reflection on perceptual experience, his phenomenology of perception, does not proceed at random, arbitrarily. Rather, it is guided by what Merleau-Ponty intends to establish through the reflection; in other words, the very kind of reflection undertaken is dictated by what is to be established through it.

In general, Merleau-Ponty wants to establish the *primacy of perception*. In this regard we need to distinguish three issues.

First, perception is original.

That means perception is not reducible to thought, and the perceptual object is not reducible to an object of thought (something constituted by thought). Hence it must be shown by reflection that the perceptual sphere involves an opaqueness, a basis, which cannot be analyzed into something constituted by thought. Instead, this basis reveals itself as always already unaccountably there.

In the most general terms, this basis is the already established anchorage, engagement, of the subject in the world. Here "world" is to be understood not as an object of thought, or a mere sum of all things, but as the ultimate horizon from out of which all things announce themselves.

To say that the subject is anchored in the world is to say that the world is always already there, that the subject is always already situated and "knows its way around" in the midst of things. It is to say that the subject is being-in-the-world (*être au monde*), being-to or -toward the world.

Here it is evident how the kind of reflection required is dictated by what is to be established. It is not a matter of a reflection which penetrates the perceptual dimension (since to penetrate it would amount to showing that it *is* reducible to thought). Instead, there is required a reflection which in some way brings to light the opaqueness inherent in the perceptual dimension without dissolving that opaqueness. It is a matter of a reflection which reveals the world "as strange and paradoxical" and which reveals perceptual consciousness as always already present to the world, as being-in-the-world.

Second, perception is autonomous with respect to thought.

Not only is perception irreducible to thought but it also does not presuppose thought, is not in any way based on thought. Again, this will require a curious kind of reflection.

Third, perception founds thought.

That is, thought has its roots in perception; it originates out of perception and always retains its connection to perception. In general terms: reason has its roots in the pre-rational.

* * *

Now we can define more precisely the character of a phenomenology of perception: it is a transcendental reflection which proceeds in such a way as to bring to light the primacy of perceptual experience. That means: it brings to light the opaque, already established presence to the world (the presence presupposed by perception) and reveals the perceptual dimension as autonomous and founding.

This conception of a phenomenology of perception is precisely what Merleau-Ponty expresses in various ways in the Preface.

(1) Merleau-Ponty asks: "What is phenomenology?" He then proceeds to characterize phenomenology by a series of its seemingly contradictory intentions:

> Phenomenology is the study of essences—but also puts essences back into existence and takes facticity as its starting point.
> Phenomenology suspends the natural attitude—yet asserts that the world is always already there.
> Phenomenology seeks to be philosophy as "rigorous science"—yet "is also an account of 'lived' space, 'lived' time, and the 'lived' world."

In all these respects, the apparent conflict is simply an expression of that fundamental tension which we saw emerging in *The Structure of Behavior* and which we have expressed in several ways:

First, as the tension between consciousness as universal milieu and consciousness as rooted in subordinated dialectics (physical and vital orders).

Second, as the tension involved in a conception of a philosophy which, on the one hand, is transcendental and, on the other, preserves the truth of naturalism, the "dependence of mind."

So it is the tension inherent in the concept of *finite consciousness* and *finite philosophizing.*

Third, as a tension with respect to phenomenology itself. On the one hand, phenomenology is transcendental and regards everything as it is for consciousness. On the other hand, phenomenology does not dissolve the object into something merely constituted by consciousness but rather brings to light an already established anchorage of consciousness in the world: the fact of its being-in-the-world.

(2) Merleau-Ponty proceeds to distinguish phenomenology from science and from traditional transcendental philosophy (and the idealism to which this

leads). He does so by underscoring again the primacy of our perceptual engagement in the world.

Phenomenology seeks to return to our immediate experience of the world. As such, it undercuts or suspends science, because "the entire universe of science is built upon the lived world" (PP viii, ii–iii). Science is always a second-order expression of this underlying lived experience: "To return to the things themselves is to return to this world which is prior to knowledge in the usual sense, of which knowledge always *speaks*, and in relation to which every scientific determination is abstract, merely signitive, and dependent" (PP ix, iii).

By its return to the lived world, phenomenology is also entirely different than idealism, which seeks to reconstruct the world from the synthesizing activity of the subject. Phenomenology does not construct the world from a synthetic, judging activity and so does not exhibit the world as something constituted. Rather, for phenomenology, the world is always already there, prior to any judging activity.

(3) Thus the primary effort of phenomenology is devoted to letting the world as always already there come to light. "Phenomenology even directs all its effort toward rejoining this naive contact with the world and granting it, finally, philosophical status" (PP vii, i).

It is in terms of this task that Merleau-Ponty interprets Husserl's reductions. Thus, the phenomenological reduction is executed not in order to trace everything back to the constitutive activity of consciousness but rather to bring to light the fact that the world is always already there. According to Merleau-Ponty: "precisely in order to see the world and to grasp it as paradoxical, we must break our familiarity with it, and . . . this break teaches us nothing but the unmotivated upsurge of the world. The greatest lesson of the reduction is the impossibility of a complete reduction" (PP xiv, viii).

In terms we have used earlier, Merleau-Ponty's reflection is one designed to bring to light the opaqueness, the "always already there" at the heart of perceptual experience. And reflection can do this only if it is *incomplete* reflection: only if a complete reduction is impossible.

(4) The Preface concludes with some cryptic remarks regarding the character of phenomenological philosophy in general. Specifically, Merleau-Ponty suggests how a philosophy which proceeds in the way described must understand itself. Here we can distinguish two issues:

The general issue is that philosophy is always a problem for itself. That means philosophy, versus science, cannot take itself for granted and defer the justification of its method and standpoint to some higher discipline. "Philosophy itself must not take itself for granted" (PP xiv, ix).

Philosophy must, then, seek to give an account of itself; philosophical interrogation must simultaneously be self-interrogation:

Phenomenology, as revelatory of the world, rests on itself or, rather, provides its own foundation. On the other hand, all knowledge in the usual sense is erected upon a "base" of postulates and, ultimately, upon our communication with the world as the first establishment of rationality. Philosophy, as radical reflection, denies itself this resource as a matter of principle. Yet, since it too is in history, it too utilizes the world and constituted reason. It must therefore address to itself the question it addresses to all knowledge, and so it will constantly double back on itself and will be, as Husserl says, an infinite dialogue or infinite meditation. Insofar as it remains faithful to its intention, phenomenology will never know where it is heading. (PP xx–xxi, xvi)

In other words, philosophy can never take its standpoint, its own beginning, for granted but instead must continually return to an interrogation of its own beginnings. That is, philosophy involves a continual return to beginnings. (Husserl called himself a "perpetual beginner.")

Second, the more specific issue is this: what does establishing the primacy of perception entail with respect to philosophical self-understanding? That is, if, having established the primacy of perception, we execute a return to beginnings, what can we then say about the beginnings, about the character of a philosophical standpoint? That is what Merleau-Ponty is anticipating at the end of the Preface.

Recall that Merleau-Ponty proposes to return to things as they present themselves perceptually—primarily on the grounds that whatever we come to know about things is based on this experience. It seems so obvious that one wonders how philosophy took 2,500 years to get around to making this return.

Indeed it is obvious that our primary access to things is through perception. But what is not obvious is that all of our knowledge of things is positively based on our perceptual experience. Instead, almost the whole tradition has argued that perception is only a means to knowledge, a means to be ignored once we attain to knowledge. That is, the tradition has supposed that there is a true order of things which knowledge mirrors. Perception, on the contrary, is only a confused image of this true order and is relevant only as a means by which to make the ascent to knowledge.

Now Merleau-Ponty is proposing to establish that the originary order is that of the perceptual dimension, that "the only *logos* that preexists is the world itself," that the originary order (*logos*) is not an order genuinely accessible to thought alone but is rather the *logos* of the sensible world.

Accordingly, thought—specifically philosophical thought—is not a mirroring of an objective order above and beyond the order (*logos*) inherent in the perceptual dimension: "The phenomenological world is not the mere explicitation of a preexistent being but is the founding of being; philosophy is not the reflection of a preexistent truth but, like art, is the bringing of truth into being. It will be asked how this bringing into being is *possible*, and whether it does not rejoin a

Reason preexisting in things. But the only *logos* that preexists is the world itself" (PP xx, xv).

In other words, thought is founded on perception and simply establishes at the level of judgment the *logos* of the perceptual world. Thought does not initiate us into a preexisting order of truth which would be only poorly reflected at the level of perception.

So, we can say that the establishment, by philosophical thought, of the primacy of perception and hence of the founded character of thought, recoils upon the very character of that philosophical thought: "Here, for the first time, the philosopher's meditation is sufficiently conscious not to expect to find its own results already realized in the world prior to that meditation" (PP xx, xv). That is, philosophical thought does not rediscover an already existing order of truth but rather simply carries over to the level of judgment the *logos* of the sensible world.

B. The Introduction of the *Phenomenology of Perception*: Traditional Prejudices and the Return to the Phenomena

The title of the Introduction already raises questions. What are these traditional prejudices? Why do they call for a return to the phenomena? What is the character of this return?

Before these questions can be addressed, some broad, general issues need to be taken up. Let us begin with what I term the "radical character" of philosophical thought. I mean thereby the peculiar self-reflection involved in philosophical thought, the fact that philosophy must account for itself. That can be seen by contrasting philosophy with science. Physics cannot, by its available methods, describe and determine its own nature. Rather, it must appeal to philosophical thought, which delimits the region of the objects of physics, the constitution of that region, and the appropriate methods for investigating the things in the region.

But what about philosophy itself? It cannot appeal to something more fundamental through which its nature would be determined. Rather, it must account for itself. What does this self-accounting amount to? Often it has been conceived as a reenactment, a retracing, even an imitation of something already constituted, established, preexistent. But then the danger arises that its own—the philosopher's own—individual and historical standpoint will be canceled, as if one could jump over one's own shadow. Is such a manner of self-accounting still possible today?

Can we understand thought in general as an imitation of the real being of objects and philosophical thought as an imitation of some special region of objects? There are two difficulties standing in the way of such a conception of philosophy:

(1) There is no special region of objects in reference to which philosophy could be defined. If philosophy were tied to a specific region of objects, then in the end philosophy could not account for itself, for its being related to a specific region. Accordingly, philosophy has *no* "subject-matter."

(2) What can we say about "real objects"? We gain access to objects only through perception, we have access only to perceptual objects, and so-called real objects (for instance, objects as thematized by science) are never more than sheer extrapolations and constructions—they are ideal.

The outcome of these difficulties is this: philosophy cannot account for itself as imitation or reproduction of some ideal model. Rather, reflection is creative; there is no model. As Merleau-Ponty says in the Preface, already cited: "Here, for the first time, the philosopher's meditation is sufficiently conscious not to expect to find its own results already realized in the world prior to that meditation."

Furthermore, philosophical thought never escapes its own standpoint, its facticity. Hence philosophical thinking is situated, historical, a response. It can never divest itself of its origins, never be perfectly self-transparent. It can never fully take account of itself. It involves, as Husserl says, an infinite meditation.

This is the situation in which we as philosophers find ourselves: our situation is one prescribing that philosophy can take place only as situated, only from out of our situation. We are involved in a kind of *situational circularity*.

One can of course deny the situational character of philosophical thought. And any person who chooses that path cannot be refuted. We could at most say, as Merleau-Ponty says of a variety of this way of thinking, that such a person suffers from a kind of mental blindness. Merleau-Ponty, on the contrary, places himself squarely within the contemporary philosophical situation, and his thinking is a response to that situation.

Even if there is no preestablished objective order which our experience or thought copies, we can nevertheless say at least this much about experience and the world it discloses: we must take our stance within experience. We cannot begin with an objective order and reconstruct experience from it. Rather, we must try to see how something like an objective order can arise out of experience: how there can be an in-itself for-us. And experience here means, first of all, perception, for it is in perception that the world first opens up for us.

Empiricism and intellectualism, which Merleau-Ponty regards as the two principal modes of thought in modern times, are both guilty of the same error: they take as their point of departure the idea of a preestablished objective order. Hence experience—in particular, perception—becomes for them re-creation or imitation. It is thus that they have missed the phenomenon of perception. Merleau-Ponty's response to the contemporary situation is a *phenomenology* of perception.

* * *

We return now to the title. With regard to the "traditional prejudices" mentioned there, in fact they derive from *one* fundamental prejudice: perception is understood by starting with the idea of a preestablished objective order of which perception is a copy. That is, perception is regarded in terms of the *logos* of object-ive thought rather than in terms of its own inherent *logos*.

The first three chapters of the Introduction expose the forms this prejudice takes in various contexts: sensation, association, the projection of memories, attention, and judgment. In each case Merleau-Ponty shows that the prejudice in favor of the objective world leads us to miss the genuine phenomenon. The final chapter of the Introduction then consolidates the results and proposes a "return to the phenomena."

(1) Sensation.

Normally, perception is distinguished from sensation. The latter is taken as the simple element (given via the sense organs) from which perception is some-how built up: either by adding sensations together (empiricism) or by super-imposing on them something else, such as a judgment or other act of thought (intellectualism).

Merleau-Ponty's position is that the concept of sensation is hopelessly inad-equate; it overlooks what is distinctive about perception. His criticism is the same one he levels against all atomism: there are no simple atoms, because any element is always related internally to the whole.

Thus the apprehension of a sense-datum, a quality, is not the apprehension of some autonomous atomic unit. Instead, sense-apprehension is bound up with the entire perceptual context. For example:

> The quality, if taken in the very experience which reveals it, is just as rich and just as obscure as the object or as the entire perceived spectacle. This section of the red carpet remains seen as red only if account is taken of the shadow which lies on it; the red quality appears only in relation to the play of light and hence only as an element of an entire spatial configuration. Furthermore, the color is a determinate one only if it covers a surface of a certain size; too small a surface can have no color quality. Finally, this red would literally not be the same if it were not the "woolly red" of a carpet. (PP 4–5, 10)

The point is that sense experience involves a richness and a contextual char-acter ignored by the concept of sensation. That is, the concept of sensation is not a description of what is immediately given but rather is an idea imposed on sense-experience in our attempt to understand it.

A question is indeed why it seems so natural to isolate a layer of pure sensa-tions in perception. Merleau-Ponty answers in terms of the "experience error," which means the following: "What we know to be in things themselves we sup-pose to be immediately in our consciousness of them. We make perception out of the perceived. And since the perceived itself is obviously accessible only through perception, we end by comprehending neither" (PP 5, 11).

As regards sensations, we know objects to be composed of bits of matter, and accordingly we suppose that our experience of these objects is composed out of corresponding bits of sensation. This error in turn points back to the "constancy hypothesis": "The objective world being given, it is assumed that it imparts to the sense-organs messages which must be inscribed, and then deciphered, so as to reproduce in us the original text. Consequently, there is, as a matter of principle, a point-by-point correspondence and constant connection between the stimulus and the elementary perception" (PP 7, 14).

This, however, is simply the attempt to begin with a preestablished objective order and reconstruct perception from it. It is that fundamental prejudice which subjects perceptual experience to a *logos* of objective thought rather than being heedful of its own inherent *logos*.

Merleau-Ponty points out especially how this prejudice leads us to overlook what is distinctive about the perceptual object inasmuch as we regard it as fully developed and determinate. Indeed, that is the character of the ideal object constructed by science; such an object has no gaps. And if I reconstruct perception from this object, then it too will have no gaps.

But in actual perception, the object is never without lacunae and always involves ambiguity, indeterminateness, and dependence on context. For instance, I may be familiar with a face without having perceived the color of the eyes. Or I can be aware of things on the edge of my visual field as "things of some sort" but not as fully determinate objects.

(2) Association.

Merleau-Ponty extends this critique to association. The empiricist, having assumed a layer of sensation, tries to compose perception by merely adding sensations together. Thus, to see a whole (a figure) simply amounts to experiencing simultaneously all the atomic sensations that form it. Then whatever else might be involved in perception (meaning, significance) is accounted for by means of the association of ideas, which brings into play past experience and specifically the images left by previous sense-impressions.

Thus empiricism assumes there is a first layer of pure sensation, merely sensed and devoid of meaning, and a second level at which sensations are linked together (associated) into a meaningful whole.

Merleau-Ponty's critique makes two points:

First, such a distinction of levels cannot be maintained. The sense-data are not independent of the way they are related. For example, suppose we try to see as things the intervals between the things and, conversely, the things as intervals. Then "there would not simply be the same elements differently combined, the same sensations differently associated, the same text invested with a different sense, the same matter in another form, but, in truth, another world" (PP 16, 23).

The same phenomenon occurs in glancing at a map and taking the contours of the bodies of water as contours of land masses. Thus there is no level at which relations are absent; whatever is given is always already bound to a context, always already submitted to the figure-ground structure.

Second, there is accordingly no level at which what is given is devoid of meaning. The given is always infused with meaning. And association, far from accounting for meaning, rather presupposes such meaning. The resemblances that are supposed to bear the association are subsequent to the supposed work of association:

> If I am walking along a beach toward a stranded ship, and if the funnel and mast are blending into the trees bordering the dune, there will come a moment in which these appendages vigorously rejoin the ship and rivet themselves back on to it. As I was approaching, I did not perceive any resemblances or proximities, precisely that which is supposed to unite the entire superstructure of the ship in one integral configuration. I merely felt that the aspect of the object was about to change, that something was imminent in this tension the way a storm is imminent in clouds. Then the spectacle suddenly reorganized itself, giving satisfaction to my imprecise expectation. Afterwards I did recognize, as justifications for the change, the resemblance and contiguity of what I now identify as "stimuli"—that is, the most determinate phenomena, obtained at close range, of which I compose the "true" world. (PP 17, 24)

(3) Projection of memories.

The same results formulated for the concept of association apply also to the presumed role of memory in perception. It is argued, for example, that since in visual perception not everything is visibly given—in reading I do not actually see all the letters of a word—the gaps must be filled in by a projection of memories.

But, here again, the account presupposes what it is meant to account for: "Prior to all contributions of memory, what is seen must here and now organize itself in such a way as to offer me a tableau in which I can recognize my previous experiences. Thus the appeal to memories presupposes what it is supposed to explain: the organization of what is given, the imposition of a meaning onto a sensuous chaos" (PP 19, 27).

In opposition, Merleau-Ponty maintains that "upon returning to the phenomena we find, as a fundamental stratum, a whole already pregnant with an irreducible meaning and not lacunary sensations, amid which memories are supposed to insert themselves" (PP 21–22, 29).

And that is, in general, what Merleau-Ponty wants to show in all three cases considered thus far: when we attend to perceptual experience we find, not a mass of sensations devoid of meaning, but wholes and structures always already charged with meaning. In other words, structure and meaning do not originate only at a level above that of perception proper, above the level of our perceptual contact with things. Instead, perception is an autonomous locus of the emergence of meaning.

(4) Attention.

We have said that there is fundamental prejudice preventing us from seeing the originary character of perception. This prejudice amounts to holding that perception is to be understood by starting with the idea of an objective order of things. This prejudice is characteristic not only of empiricism but also of intellectualism. Merleau-Ponty proceeds to show that by considering attention.

Both empiricism and intellectualism assume the object is given in perception as something completely determinate and unambiguous, an "image" of the ideal object found in science. The fact that perceptual objects are not, in fact, normally presented in this way is regarded as a result of inattention. Thus both empiricism and intellectualism collapse the distinction between the ideal object and the perceptual object by introducing the concept of attention.

More specifically, empiricism—on the basis of the constancy hypothesis— insists that sensations (from which the ideal object is reconstructed) are there whether we attentively perceive them or not. Attention is a searchlight aimed at preexisting sensations.

As to intellectualism, it regards the object (the intelligible structure of the object) as constituted by consciousness, not as something external. But the result is the same: here too the fully developed, determinate, unambiguous object is present to consciousness (since consciousness constitutes it), and attention is simply a matter of explicating, taking note of, what is already there.

So what is common to both these views is that attention in the final analysis has no essential work to perform. Attention does not institute any new relationships but merely provides clearness regarding what is already instituted. But, if this is so, it is difficult to understand how an object could ever call forth an act of attention. Such a "calling forth" would presumably require some intrinsic connection between the object and the act called forth.

For empiricism, there are no such intrinsic connections, whereas for intellectualism all connections with all objects are intrinsic. That is to say, for empiricism, nothing would seem capable of eliciting an act of attention; for intellectualism, everything would be equally capable of it: "Empiricism does not see that we need to know what we are looking for, or else we would not be seeking it; and intellectualism fails to see that we need to be ignorant of what we are looking for, or else, again, we would not be seeking. . . . Both are oblivious to that circumscribed ignorance, that still 'empty'—though already determinate—intention which is attention itself" (PP 28, 36).

For Merleau-Ponty, attention is creative: it is a transformation of the perceptual field, "a new way for consciousness to be present to its objects" (PP 29, 37). Accordingly, the act of attention takes place from out of a prior presence of the object, against a background of "circumscribed ignorance": "To pay attention is not merely to shed greater light on certain preexisting givens; it is to bring about a new articulation of them by taking them as *figures*. . . . Attention is the active constitution of a new object which thematizes and makes explicit what had been offered up to then merely as an indeterminate horizon" (PP 30, 38–39).

Here we have one of the first instances in which Merleau-Ponty specifically describes a conscious act in its inseparable relation to a lower, lived, preconscious level, that is, in terms of its relation to its constitutive history.

Merleau-Ponty concludes his discussion of attention by relating his account to this all-important general theme: "Consciousness must be placed in the presence of its unreflective life in things and awakened to its own history which it was forgetting—that is the true role of philosophical reflection, and that is the path to a true theory of attention" (PP 31, 40).

(5) Judgment.

The concept of judgment is central to the intellectualistic account of perception. Judgment is "what sensation lacks to become perception" (PP 32, 40). There are numerous instances in which what we see does not agree with what we know to be actually imprinted on the retina. Judgment is then invoked to account for the disagreement.

For example, I have two eyes, they present me with two sets of visual data, and I ought to see objects double. But, since I do not, judgment or interpretation must intervene between the sensation and the perception, in some way combining the two sets of data into a single visual image. Thus perception becomes in effect the interpretation of sensation.

Merleau-Ponty objects to this collapsing of the distinction between perception and judgment. He offers the example of a cube drawn on paper, the Necker cube. The two ways of perceiving it ought to be merely a matter of judgment, since the sensations remain the same. But this is not so. There is an intuitive realization which I must *await* before the organization of the figure changes.

Merleau-Ponty insists that the distinction (perception versus judgment, prepredicative versus predicative) is to be retained. But he does not set about giving a theory of judgment such as would be necessary to explicate the distinction fully. Instead, for present purposes, Merleau-Ponty simply sketches the main point of the distinction, namely, the primacy of perception with respect to judgment: "to perceive in the full sense of the word . . . is not to judge but is instead to grasp a meaning immanent in the sensible prior to all judgment. The phenomenon of true perception thus offers a meaning that inheres in the signs, and judgment is merely an optional expression of that meaning" (PP 35, 44).

Accordingly, it is again a question of restoring the primacy and richness of perceptual experience.

* * *

The first three chapters of the Introduction expose the prejudice operative in traditional theories of perception and thereby restore to perceptual experience its richness, its structure, and its capacity to originate meaning. They restore to it the mystery of which it was robbed when traditional analyses reduced it to the mere reception of sense-data.

Thus these chapters open up beneath the level of explicit acts of judgment, attention, memory, and association what Merleau-Ponty calls a "phenomenal field." It is with the exploration of this field that the phenomenology of perception in the proper sense commences.

Before proceeding to this commencement, however, Merleau-Ponty relates his project to a more general issue.

We have spoken of Merleau-Ponty's philosophy as engaged, situated, a response to the contemporary situation. Merleau-Ponty now indicates in what way it is a response to the situation brought about by the course philosophy and science have followed since the beginning of the modern era, a development which has reached a crisis point in our time.

Especially important in this development is the way it has been sustained throughout by an unquestioning faith in perception, the way science and philosophy have understood themselves as amplifications of what already takes place in perception. So we must see what it is in perception that (especially) science claims merely to extend.

There is in perception a directedness toward a "truth in itself." We see such directedness in the "synthetic character" of perception. That is, in perception we find:

(1) the past coordinated with the present (transcendence of individual moments),
(2) incomplete, initial knowledge of things synthesized with what is discovered in further exploration, and
(3) my perceptual knowledge coordinated with that of others so that we come to share a common world.

Thus perception harbors an inherent movement beyond the thing momentarily given toward an object progressively less relative to an individual perceptual act. Science simply extends this tendency by severing all relations between the object and perception—by making the object an in-itself. The object is regarded not in terms of its genesis in perception but rather, to use the words of Lachelier, as a network of general properties.

In the course of such a development it was inevitable that this way of determining objects in general would eventually be applied also to the body, since from this objective standpoint the body loses that distinctive character which at the level of perception radically distinguishes it from other things.

Finally, in order to preserve the autonomy of the subject, subjectivity has to be entirely withdrawn from the body and placed in a sphere totally discontinuous with nature: "Thus, while the living body became an exterior without interior, subjectivity became an interior without exterior, a disinterested spectator" (PP 56, 68).

Whatever the situation today, the fact remains that this was a *natural* development: "science is merely pursuing uncritically the ideal of knowledge prefigured in the perceived thing" (PP 56, 69). Otherwise expressed, perception itself is the source of the temptation leading us to overlook it in favor of the scientific object.

But what is the situation today? What are we today to say of this development and its outcome? Merleau-Ponty is explicit: "Now this philosophy is unraveling right before our eyes." He continues:

> More generally, what has become problematic is the idea of a universe of thought or a universe of values, wherein all thinking lives are supposed to meet and be reconciled. Nature *is* not, in itself, geometric; it merely appears so—to a selective observer who confines himself to the macrocosmic data. Human society *is* not a community of rational minds; it could be understood so only in favored countries. . . . The experience of chaos, both on the speculative level and on the other one, invites us to see rationalism in a historical perspective, . . . to seek a philosophy which could make comprehensible the advent of reason in a world not made by reason, and to prepare the vital substructure without which reason and freedom are precarious and hollow. We will now no longer say that perception is incipient science but, instead, that classical science is perception which has forgotten its origins, perception taken as already complete. The first philosophical act would therefore be a return to the lived world, on this side of the objective world, since it is there that we might grasp the rights as well as the limits of the objective world and might restore to things their concrete physiognomy, to organisms their own proper way of relating to the world, and to subjectivity its inherence in history. (PP 56–57, 69)

Merleau-Ponty is referring to contemporary man's experience of the "fragility" of reason: reason has its roots in the pre-rational, and since this pre-rational is never simply absorbed or eliminated, it can and does break through so as to destroy reason.

In particular, scientific reason is rooted in pre-scientific perceptual experience. But precisely by its uncritical allegiance to perception, science loses sight of its roots and even pretends to abolish them. Perception comes to be regarded not as an original and autonomous ground but merely as a primitive form of science.

Merleau-Ponty suggests that when reason forgets its roots, the pre-rational eventually "reasserts" itself ("the experience of chaos") so as to destroy reason.

What is called for by this situation is a retrieval of these roots and a renewal of reason from out of such a retrieval. What is called for is a return to origins.

C. Part One of the *Phenomenology of Perception*: The Body

i. Prologue. Experience and Objective Thought.
The Problem of the Body

In the Prologue, "Experience and Objective Thought. The Problem of the Body," Merleau-Ponty brings more clearly into view the gap between perceptual experience and objective thought and proposes an interrogation of the body for the purpose of approaching the problems arising from that gap.

We have spoken of the gap: inherent in perception is a natural tendency toward objectivity, toward the transcendence of all standpoints. Science claims merely to complete this natural tendency. But Merleau-Ponty maintains that science is uncritical and that its "completion" of this tendency involves serious difficulties. So we need to see the precise character of this tendency and the way the attempt by science to complete it is a falsification of the movement as it occurs in perception.

Perception is perspectival; things present only profiles to us. Yet we never identify an object with any of its profiles; we never identify the object itself with its appearance from a particular perspective. Instead, the object itself is what reveals itself (always partially) through the various profiles it offers. So perception is enclosed in a perspective, yet the profile is perceived *as* a profile *of* an object, and thus perception escapes its perspective and opens up onto a relatively stable world of things.

The problem is to determine the character of this objectifying movement. Specifically, what makes it possible for perception to escape confinement in a perspective and yet still be bound to it? That is, what makes possible the transition from the momentarily presented profile to a stable world of things? Merleau-Ponty's answer is that the horizonal character of perceptual experience makes the transition possible. Accordingly, we need to examine the horizonal structures, spatial and temporal ones.

(1) Spatial horizons. All perception involves the figure-ground, object-horizon structure, including an outer and inner horizon.

(a) Outer horizon. When I concentrate my attention on an object, that object always stands out as a figure against a background of other objects. This outer horizon of other objects remains on the fringe of my perceptual field, and it guarantees the identity of thematic object throughout exploration.

(b) Inner horizon. This is a horizonal structure within the thematic object itself. The profile presented by the object stands out as a figure against a background of the totality of other profiles the object could present to other viewpoints. I can, of course, change my position so as to have these profiles (the inner horizon) directly given rather than merely anticipated.

Merleau-Ponty especially stresses the way the inner and outer horizons are connected. In the first place, peripheral objects (forming the outer horizon) are grasped in terms of their reference to the thematic object: "To look at an object is to inhabit it and to grasp, from that vantage point, all things according to the face they turn toward it" (PP 68, 82). Furthermore, the thematic object is grasped not only in the profile it presents to me but also in the profiles it presents to the peripheral objects. For example, when I look at a desk, it is perceived as presenting not only the profile I can see but is also grasped in terms of the profiles it presents to the walls, the door, and so on. In other words, the inner horizon refers to the outer. Various profiles that make up the inner horizon are precisely profiles that would be presented to various perspectives occupied by the things constituting the outer horizon.

So, then, if we begin with a particular given profile, it refers us to a multiplicity of profiles (inner horizon), which in turn is linked up with an outer horizon, that is to say, with a whole system of objects: "Thus I can see an object insofar as objects form a system or a world, insofar as each object takes the other ones round about it as spectators of its hidden aspects and as guarantors of the permanence of those aspects" (PP 68, 82–83).

(2) Temporal horizons.

Just as spatial horizons allow me to transcend my particular spatial perspective and hence, in some sense, to see the object from everywhere, so the horizonal structure of temporality allows me to escape confinement in the present moment and in some sense to see the object from all points of time: "Each moment of time calls all the others as its witnesses; its very occurrence shows 'how matters were supposed to turn out' and 'how they will end up.' Each present definitively founds a point of time which solicits recognition from all the others, and the object is therefore seen from all times, just as it is seen from all places, and by the same means, the horizon-structure" (PP 69, 83).

Accordingly, through these horizonal structures (both spatial and temporal), through the synthetic connections they establish, perception escapes the confines of what is merely given momentarily and in one profile. Perception is ushered into a domain of objectivity where objects are seen from all directions and from all times.

Yet this objectivity in perception is *not* the objectivity of scientific thought. For, no matter how much the horizonal structures may direct perception toward all facets of the object at all times, the object is nevertheless thematically given only with respect to a single profile and in a single moment. I am directed toward other profiles and other moments, but I never have them fully in my grasp. For instance, I retain the past, but imperfectly; there is a "shading off" so that the more remote past is no longer at all in my grasp.

Through the horizonal structures, I am directed toward the absolute standpoint of objectivity. As a perceptual subject, however, I never occupy that absolute standpoint: "the synthesis of horizons is merely a presumptive one" (PP 70, 84). Hence the object remains incomplete and indeterminate, and this character of the seen object radically distinguishes it from the scientific object. The movement, inherent in perception, toward objectivity is necessarily incomplete.

Now, it is precisely this necessary incompleteness which objective science simply abolishes. It simply posits as completed what perception can never complete; it simply and uncritically assumes the standpoint which perception can never attain. Objects become objects in themselves (totally determinate), and we completely lose sight of their connection with and emergence out of perception, out of the indeterminately perceived object. Eventually even the human body becomes merely another such object: "Thus is formed 'objective' thought (in Kierkegaard's sense), the thinking of common sense and of science, which finally makes us lose contact with perceptual experience, of which it is nevertheless the result and the natural prolongation" (PP 71, 86).

ii. Part One of the *Phenomenology of Perception*: Chapter 1. The Body as Object and Mechanistic Physiology

The body is a decisive point in the transition from perception to objective thought. Science, in objectifying, is not content simply to objectify things. Rather, having arisen out of perception, science wants then to "close the circle" by bringing perception itself within the objective order. It wants to interpret perception as an objective event, as a causal event in an object, the body. Thus it is essential for science to objectify the body.

In other terms, this is an attempt by objective thought to absorb totally into itself (and hence abolish) its roots, to absorb the pre-rational into the rational. For perception (and even for classical psychology), there are, however, certain characteristics of the body that are incompatible with a conception of it as a mere object. Chapter 2 discusses these:

First, my body is always there, always perceived, even though it is generally marginal to my perception. Unlike other things, which are contingently present, the absence of one's body is inconceivable.

Second, my body, like other objects, does involve a certain perspectivity, but in the case of the body the perspectivity is different. The body is a perspective that can never be varied. The body is the fundamental perspective from which all objects are observed, but it cannot, in the strict sense, be observed itself.

So, for perceptual experience the body is distinctive. But objective thought does not take these features seriously and regards them as simply pertaining to our representation of the body, not to the body itself. The body itself is just another object.

Merleau-Ponty wants to show how the objective conception of the body collapses and how through this collapse we are led to withdraw the body from the objective order. Furthermore, the body, in being withdrawn from the objective order, will carry along with it the things to which it is intentionally linked. Hence Merleau-Ponty proposes to reverse, to "undo," the objectification established by science. The entire objective order will be seen to collapse, and in its place we will discover the perceiving (bodily) subject and the perceived world.

In fact, the withdrawal of the body from the objective world has already been accomplished in *The Structure of Behavior*. We saw there that behavior is not a causal process in the body; the body is not a passive recipient of stimuli. Even simple reflex behavior involves a global organizing and structuring by the organism. Account has to be taken of the way the organism as a whole meets the stimulus and elaborates it. The stimulus is not a cause of a response but already involves a response.

So *The Structure of Behavior* retrieves the nonobjective body, the body as contributing to the constitution of things or, in other words, the "subjectivized" body. Merleau-Ponty's task in the *Phenomenology of Perception* is to develop this conception of the body and especially to work out the relation of the body to things (world) and to consciousness. Chapter 1 is devoted to sketching the general character of these relations. More specifically, this chapter initiates two central tasks:

(1) To reveal the body as the vehicle of our inherence in the world
(2) To show how in general the body is related to the level of conscious existence, how bodily life is related to personal life.

(1) Body and world.

Merleau-Ponty deals with the relation of the body to the world by appealing to the example of the phantom limb. He focuses on the circumstance that the phantom limb is neither a product of consciousness (not something psychological) nor a product of the body as thing (not something physiological). Indeed, both kinds of factors are involved but in a complex way.

The phantom limb cannot be explained in purely physiological terms; psychological factors are involved. For example, the phantom limb often appears in the position it had at the moment of injury, and so memory is involved. Also, emotions or circumstances which recall those in which the injury was received may occasion the sudden appearance of a phantom limb.

Yet the phantom limb cannot be explained in purely psychological terms, for the severance of the nerves from the stump to the brain eliminates the phantom limb.

There are both psychological and physiological factors involved. Accordingly, the phenomenon of the phantom limb has to be understood in relation to a dimension which is neither thing nor consciousness and yet is in some way both. Merleau-Ponty calls this dimension "being-in-the-world." The term refers to a pre-objective, pre-conscious anchorage, engagement, in the world.

Merleau-Ponty then interprets the phantom limb as an implicit denial of a mutilation which, if acknowledged, would disrupt this anchorage in the world:

> What in us refuses mutilation and incapacitation is an ego engaged in a certain physical and interhuman world, an ego that continues to strain toward its world despite disabilities or amputations and so, to this extent, does not recognize them *de jure*. The refusal of the disability is merely the reverse side of our adherence to a world; it is the implicit negation of whatever opposes the natural movement which throws us into our tasks, into our cares, into our situation, into our familiar horizons. To have a phantom arm is to remain open to all the actions of which the arm alone is capable; it is to retain the practical field that was possessed prior to the mutilation. (PP 81–82, 97)

What is the character of this anchorage? Merleau-Ponty does not elaborate except to relate it to the body: the body is the vehicle of this anchorage: "The body is the vehicle of being-in-the-world, and, for a living being, to have a body is to encounter oneself in a definite milieu, to identify oneself with certain projects, and to engage oneself in them incessantly" (PP 82, 97).

(2) Body and consciousness.

We said that the bodily anchorage in the world (being-in-the-world) is something pre-conscious. It is not something we establish as conscious subjects; it is always already established (an "absolute past"). It is in some way beneath the level of conscious activity.

Because of this, Merleau-Ponty proposes to understand the body's relation to consciousness by generalizing the concept of repression. Suppose that in the course of some enterprise, I encounter an obstacle. If I can nether surmount the obstacle nor abandon the enterprise, then I remain imprisoned in the attempt and forced to renew it constantly. This attempt gradually comes to dominate all my activities and becomes a kind of abstraction, a margin of impersonal existence, surrounding my personal life. That is how repression operates.

The point is that the body is just this kind of general, impersonal, and anonymous existence. It is an "inborn complex." The body is a kind of impersonal existence beneath the level of conscious existence and of personal acts. The body is a kind of margin of anonymous existence which is taken for granted and by which we are already engaged in the world and "know our way around" in the world. The body is a level of general existence flowing on beneath personal existence and sustaining that personal existence while at the same time compromising it.

> Most of the time personal existence represses the organism without being able to surpass it or to renounce itself—that is, without being able to reduce the organism to itself or itself to the organism. Even while I am crushed under the weight of my sorrow and completely occupied by my affliction, my gaze already wanders through the scene before me, interests itself insidiously in some gleaming object, and resumes its autonomous existence. . . . Personal existence is intermittent, and when the tide ebbs, my former decision can give my life no more than a forced significance. . . . The specific past which is our body can be assumed and appropriated by an individual life only because that life has never transcended the body but, instead, secretly nourishes it and expends there a part of its force and because the body remains the present of that life. . . . What permits us to center our existence is also what prevents us from centering it absolutely, and the anonymity of our body is inseparably freedom as well as bondage. (PP 84–85, 100–101)

This says in general that man is not a composite of consciousness and body. Instead, man is existence, and the distinction between consciousness and body is a distinction between two moments within the structure of existence. These two moments are the personal and the pre-personal (or anonymous), and they are in dynamic relation:

> Taken concretely, man is not a psyche appended to an organism but is this back-and-forth movement of existence, which now tends toward the sheer bodily and now bears itself toward personal acts. Psychological motives and bodily occasions can be integrated because a living body does not have even a single motion that would be absolutely accidental in relation to the psychic intentions, and neither is there even one psychic act whose germ or general adumbration is not to be found in the physiological substructures. (PP 88, 104)

* * *

What are we to make of Merleau-Ponty's procedure here and indeed throughout much of the *Phenomenology of Perception*? We saw that *The Structure of Behavior* attempts to retrieve the living body, the nonobjective, subjectivized body. The result is that behavior can no longer be regarded in terms of "worldly causality." That is, the body cannot be understood by viewing it as a third-person process, by viewing it objectively. Instead, I have access to the living body only as I experience it: "I must leave aside the body as an object, the body *partes extra partes*, and have recourse to the body I actually experience. . . . I cannot comprehend the function of the living body except by carrying out that function myself" (PP 75, 90).

Yet how does Merleau-Ponty proceed? He does not describe the body as experienced but instead discusses phantom limbs. His frequent recourse to the experiences of the brain-injured soldier, Schneider, is in the same vein. Why does Merleau-Ponty proceed this way? Why does he not simply describe the body as experienced, reflect on bodily existence as lived? Why these "inferences" from various clinical cases?

Let me make a suggestion. Because the body is the vehicle of an already established anchorage in the world and because the level of bodily existence is so thoroughly taken for granted, it tends to escape our attention. So if we proceeded immediately to a description, we would in fact find very little to describe.

In other words, the dimension of bodily existence is for the most part concealed from our conscious awareness. This dimension has to be wrested from concealment and drawn into view. That is what Merleau-Ponty is attempting in his appeal to the clinical cases. He takes instances in which this preestablished anchorage in the world is threatened (phantom limb) or broken down (Schneider) and uses them to bring the anchorage into view.

It could be said that I am able to carry out the function of the living body (as demanded by Merleau-Ponty) only if I in some way already have in view what I am to carry out. It is this anticipatory view that is provided by taking up the clinical examples.

iii. Part One of the *Phenomenology of Perception*: Chapter 3. The Spatiality of the Body Proper and Motility

We have seen that Merleau-Ponty wants to subjectivize the body, withdraw it from the objective order. But the body is something spatial, and to be in space is taken as distinctive of the objective over against the subjective. So Merleau-Ponty needs to interrogate the spatiality of the body and distinguish between objective and bodily space.

The Structure of Behavior had already shown that the body cannot be regarded simply as a collection of externally related parts. The parts of the body are not spread out side by side but rather are mutually enveloped. For instance, in leaning on one's hand, bodily spatiality is polarized such that the entire body is concentrated in that hand; the other parts are not purely and simply external to it. If the body is viewed from the "inside"—in the first person rather than the third person—it presents itself as a whole, a form, a Gestalt. Merleau-Ponty relates this phenomenon to the traditional concept of the "body image."

Originally the body image was conceived merely as a product of a large number of associations, principally of kinesthetic impressions with visual images, the result of a translation of the one into the other. But that is inadequate; the body image (cf. *The Structure of Behavior*) is already presupposed by association; it makes association possible, rather than vice versa. The phantom limb, for example, presupposes an already constituted body image into which the missing limb can be incorporated.

Accordingly, a more adequate concept of the body image is needed. It is not a mere product of association, but neither can the awareness of one's own body be regarded as a merely global consciousness of the actually existing parts of the body. In the case of the phantom limb, the body image, the awareness of the habitual body, includes the phantom limb, though it is nonexistent.

Merleau-Ponty proposes, then, that the body image be conceived in terms of a directedness toward certain tasks, in terms of an orientation toward a structured situation. I am aware of my body precisely *as* a directedness to a familiar structured world, and the body image is a way of being-in-the-world. Therefore, the spatiality of the body is not a spatiality of position but of situation: a spatiality of involvement, engagement, in the world. Bodily space is the background against which specific gestures and aims stand out, and it is in turn polarized, oriented, by that gesture (as in leaning on a hand).

Now, a gesture or aim is always intentional; it aims at the world, specifically at some figure which itself stands out from a background or spatial horizon. That is to say, in an intentional act, there is always a double spatial horizon: the horizon of bodily space and the one of external space.

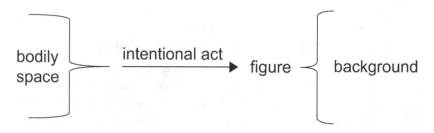

Merleau-Ponty is trying to establish this double spatial horizon and thereby show that the spatiality of the body is irreducible to objective space and indeed is radically original. What would happen if we tried to make this reduction? It would destroy all those distinctive spatial characteristics inherent in perceptual experience, ones expressed in the words "on," "under," "beside," and so forth. In general, the oriented character, the polarization and directionality of bodily space, would be destroyed if this space were reduced to isotropic, homogeneous, objective space.

Do we then simply need to establish two concepts of space, that of lived, bodily space and that of objective space? Merleau-Ponty answers, "No." Conceptualized, intelligible space is never anything other than objective space: "As soon as I try to thematize bodily space or elaborate its sense, I find in it only intelligible space" (PP 102, 118).

Thus objective space is precisely an intelligible, conceptualized space which has been detached from any connection with what is lived. The distinction between lived space and objective space is not a distinction between concepts but rather one between space as lived and space as known. And since space is known on the basis of our experience of it as lived, it is lived space which has the primacy. Conceptualized space is a "second-order expression" of it.

The spatiality of the body is one of situation and is bound up with the body's directedness toward, engagement in, the world. The body is spatial, not by being passively submitted to a spatial location, but rather by actively assuming space, by living its space. Accordingly, the spatiality of the body must be understood in connection with the body's way of assuming space, namely, by way of action and movement, by way of "motility."

* * *

The remainder of Chapter 3 is then concerned with uncovering the basis of bodily motility, that is to say, with uncovering the primordial bodily engagement in the world, being-in-the-world, or what Merleau-Ponty will in this context call the "projective function."

The structure of the argument—here as everywhere—is dictated by the general problematic and outlook and specifically by the two theses we have already identified: transcendentalism and the primacy of perception. The argument then proceeds in four stages:

(1) Identification of the projective function
(2) Refutation of the empiricist interpretation of the projective function and thus the establishment of a transcendental interpretation
(3) Modification of the transcendental interpretation through the thesis of the primacy of perception
(4) Phenomenological interpretation of the projection function (being-in-the-world)

(1) The projective function.
The body is always already established in its movement in the world. How, then, is this pre-conscious dimension to be disclosed? Merleau-Ponty proposes to

penetrate it by considering an example of "pathological motility," a case in which the body's anchorage in the world is disrupted.

The case is that of Schneider. It will serve, first, for identifying, disengaging, that primordial being-in-the-world which Merleau-Ponty is calling the projective function. Subsequently it will serve to guide Merleau-Ponty's attempt to interpret the character of this function.

Let us consider Schneider's relevant symptoms. With his eyes shut he is unable to perform abstract movements, that is, movements not done in the context of some ordinary task, movements done simply on command. He can indeed perform movements in the abstract, but only if he is allowed to watch the limb used or go through some preparatory movements involving his whole body. He does perform quite accurately the ordinary concrete movements of his habitual life.

Merleau-Ponty's general interpretation of the case is as follows. Schneider's difficulty lies in the fact that his bodily space is given only as a matrix of habitual action, only in terms of familiar tasks. What he is unable to do is to re-constitute bodily space in terms of an abstract command. When faced with the assignment of performing a movement in the abstract, he sets out with a series of preparatory movements which attempt to *substitute* for a kind of bodily presence he lacks. He cannot immediately place himself within a virtual (merely experimental) situation. To place his body in such a situation, he must first objectify his body (find his hand) and then explicitly relate the virtual situation to his actual one.

For concrete movement, the background is the habitual world already actually given; in this context, Schneider has no difficulty. But for abstract movement the background must be built up; a virtual or human space must be *projected*. And that is precisely what Schneider lacks, a bodily, motor project, a bodily orientation, capable of building up a background for movement:

"What he lacks is neither motility nor thought, and here we are invited to recognize—between movement as a third person process and thought as a representation of movement—an anticipatory grasp of the goal, a grasp assured by the body itself as a motor power. That is, we are invited to acknowledge a 'motor project,' a 'motor intentionality,' without which an abstract command remains a dead letter" (PP 110, 128).

Thus the problem arises: What is this motor intentionality, this bodily intentionality? What is the projection or projective function by which a background is built up?

(2) Empiricism.

Merleau-Ponty considers at great length the explanations empiricism and intellectualism give of the projective function. Empiricism derives this function from sensory contents; intellectualism makes it an act of consciousness independent of those contents.

Empiricism attempts a realistic interpretation which in effect denies any such special projective function. The empiricist would remind us that Schneider has serious visual disorders resulting from a brain injury in war. He cannot perform abstract movement simply because his visual representation is impaired.

This interpretation thus identifies the projective function with the possession of certain sensory contents. But any such derivation of being-in-the-world from the mere possession of sensory contents has been refuted in *The Structure of Behavior*. So we do not now need to go through the argument as given in the *Phenomenology of Perception*.

(3) Transcendentalism.

We come then to the other alternative: that of transcendental philosophy. For this interpretation, the projective function is distinct from sensory contents. It is rather that which unifies the contents around an intelligible core and gives us thereby a unified, meaningful, coherent world. Thus the projective function is a sense-giving act of consciousness. Consciousness constitutes the world in which we are engaged.

But here as always such a presumably transparent, transcendental consciousness must be confronted with its rootedness in its constitutive history, its genesis from out of the "lived." That is the thesis of the primacy of perception.

In particular, Merleau-Ponty points out that if our world were simply the transparent product of our own constituting activity, it would be impossible to conceive how anything such as error, sickness, or madness could ever separate us from the world. That is, the human subject would be totally transparent to himself, incarnation would in effect be dissolved, and we would have to say: "The madman, *behind* his ravings, his obsessions, and his delusions, *knows* that he is raving, that he is giving in to an obsession, that he is deluded; therefore he *is* not mad, *he thinks he is*. Hence, all is for the best, and madness is nothing more than bad will" (PP 125, 146).

(4) Phenomenological interpretation.

Merleau-Ponty insists that the projective function is neither reducible to sensory contents nor totally independent of them. Instead, the relation is that of *Fundierung* ("founding"). The projective function rests on the sensory functions (perception) yet takes up and transforms those functions in a way that cannot be accounted for solely in terms of sensory contents. (This is the same relation as that between levels as worked out in *The Structure of Behavior*.) According to Merleau-Ponty, the symbolic, that is, projective, function

rests on vision as on a ground—not because vision would be its cause, but because vision is that gift of nature which Spirit is ordained to utilize in a way that exceeds what might have been hoped, on which it is to confer a radically new meaning, yet of which it itself has need, not only for its incarnation, but in order to be at all. The form integrates the content to such an extent that the latter eventually appears to be a mere mode of the form itself, and the historical preparations of thought appear to be a ruse of Reason disguised as Nature. On the other hand, however, even in its intellectual sublimation, the content remains radically contingent. (PP 127, 147–48)

In the most general terms, this means that the world, as a structured meaningful context we take for granted, is not simply projected by a transcendental subject untouched by things. Rather, this projecting relies on (is founded on) the sensory content the world offers us. That is why a destruction of visual content can be a factor in Schneider's difficulty with abstract movement.

A subject does not, strictly speaking, project a world, neither the primary world of nature nor the secondary worlds of culture and thought. Instead, the subject is *always already* in a world: "An actual subject must first of all have a world or be engaged in the world—that is to say, the subject must uphold, round about itself, a system of significations whose correspondences, relations, and connections do not need to be made explicit in order to be utilized" (PP 129, 150).

It is in such a context that things have their familiarity and are recognized immediately, so that we do not need to interpret them. At the same time, we can say that the world is "built up" through a dialogue of subject and object, through a dialectic of form and content. This does not mean that we ever reach a point where there could be a subject without a world so that we might be able to trace out how this subject comes to have a world. Instead, it means that we can see in the case of secondary worlds how they are built up out of, carved out of, the primary world.

The key idea here is *sedimentation*. In the course of experience, certain meanings and structures (perceptual or cognitive) are established. What is constituted is then retained as an acquired basis, a springboard for further activity (for example, the act of adding requires already constituted numbers). This basis is retained as a sediment, not as something specifically remembered, but as a system of meanings that I have at my command, that I can take for granted and take up in further experience.

This character of sedimentation adheres to all the life of consciousness. All spontaneous activity takes place on the basis of an acquired sediment: "The structure of a world, with its two moments of sedimentation and spontaneity, is at the center of consciousness" (PP 130, 152). Furthermore: "Inasmuch as consciousness is consciousness of things only by leaving behind a trace of its activity, and inasmuch as consciousness, in order to think an object, must build on a previously constructed 'world of thought,' there is always a depersonalization at the heart of consciousness" (PP 137, 159).

The depersonalization is the sedimented acquisition which was once the object of active synthesis but is now taken for granted and not personally synthesized when taken up into a higher formation.

In general, consciousness is always situated, always already in a world. Its spontaneity is always exercised on the basis of something acquired, something already constituted. The projective function is precisely that by which there is sedimentation, hence that by which we have a world. This bodily project is "an activity of projection which deposits objects all around itself, as traces of its own acts, but which still relies on these objects in order to pass on to other acts of spontaneity, and so we can then comprehend in a unitary way how every deficiency in 'contents' could have repercussions everywhere in experience" (PP 136, 159).

So Merleau-Ponty summarizes: "The life of consciousness—cognitive life, the life of desire, or perceptual life—is subtended by an 'intentional arc' which projects round about us our past, our future, our human milieu, our physical situation, our ideological situation, and our moral situation, or, rather, which makes it be that we are indeed situated in all these respects" (PP 136, 158).

We can draw two conclusions and relate the current discussion to issues we took up earlier:

(1) We said that for Merleau-Ponty consciousness is never pure transparency but rather always remains rooted in, always retains in itself, its own constitutive history. We see now how this history is retained, namely, as sedimentation, and we see that this retention is the work of the body in its projective function. And since conscious activity (spontaneity) always requires something sedimented, we see why consciousness cannot be severed from its constitutive history.

(2) Consciousness is not pure transparency, consciousness retains its own constitutive history, because consciousness is radically *incarnated*. But we see that at the end of this chapter of the *Phenomenology of Perception* Merleau-Ponty has been generalizing beyond the problem of the body. Indeed, our bodily anchorage in the world is one way—the primary way—in which we possess an already constituted basis. But it is not the only way. This same structure (sedimentation-spontaneity) is involved at every level, even at the level of thought. This suggests, then, that the problem of the body is only a particular—though indeed privileged—case of something all-pervasive, namely, the rootedness of the mind, its dependence on lower levels, the dependence that constitutes the truth of naturalism.

iv. Part One of the *Phenomenology of Perception*: Chapter 5. The Body as a Sexed Being

We have been trying to see the main dimensions of the problem of the body:

(1) The relation of the body to things: the body as the vehicle of our pre-conscious, pre-objective anchorage in the world.

(2) The relation of the body to conscious existence: the body as a level of anonymous existence, as a pre-personal substratum beneath personal life, sustaining personal life and also compromising it.

We saw how in Chapter 3 Merleau-Ponty takes up and elaborates the first of these issues. The anchorage in the world is not something the subject establishes; instead, the subject is always already in the world. This anchorage can be interrogated only in the sense that we can see its pointing back into an ongoing dialogue between the subject and things, a dialogue which "lays down" a sediment, constitutes a basis.

Furthermore, to say that the subject is always already in the world, already anchored in the world through the body, is to say that one "knows one's way around" in a world which is coherent, articulated, and familiar—and so is meaningful. It is to say that one is in touch with the context of things in such a way that things are immediately recognizable and do not first need to be interpreted (versus things as they are for Schneider).

But this means that, in the dimension of our bodily anchorage in the world, there is a constitution of meaning, "a birth of being for us." The bodily engagement is a dimension in which meaning emerges, a locus of the emergence of meaning. Thus Merleau-Ponty says at the end of Chapter 3 that we have discovered a new meaning of the word "meaning": "All meaning was understood as an act of thought, as the operation of a pure ego, and even if intellectualism is obviously superior to empiricism, it itself is incapable of accounting for the variety of our experiences, for their non-rational moments, for the contingency of the contents. The experience of the body, however, allows us insight into an imposition of meaning not accomplished by a universal constituting consciousness and thus allows us insight into a meaning which adheres to the contents themselves" (PP 147, 172).

This is the principal issue in the chapters on sexuality and on speech, namely, to work out in the concrete this new meaning of "meaning," to exhibit bodily existence as a locus of an emergence of meaning, to exhibit the *logos* of the sensible world.

But before we look at the investigations of these chapters we need a better perspective on this general issue. As regards the new meaning of "meaning," there are two main points to be established:

(1) The body is a bestower of meaning.

(2) There is a meaning which "adheres to the contents themselves." The bestowal of meaning is not a sheer projection by a subject untouched by things but, instead, is dependent on the way things present themselves. That is, the bestowal of meaning is bound up with an apprehension of meaning.

We need to see how recognition of this bestowal is a radical break with the philosophical tradition, especially with the tradition of transcendental philosophy. For the tradition, the bestowal of meaning is strictly the work of consciousness or thought, not of the body. Indeed, the tradition allows for an apprehension by the body, but it is an apprehension of mere sensory contents devoid of form or meaning.

The result is that either there is no real apprehension of meaning or this apprehension is the work of consciousness (consciousness apprehends in things the meaning it has itself bestowed on them.) Consequently, for the tradition consciousness (thought) is the locus—the only locus—where meaning emerges. The only *logos* is the *logos* of thought.

Let us see more specifically what Merleau-Ponty needs to show in order to work out a new meaning of meaning and exhibit the *logos* of the sensible world. First, he must show that the body's function is not simply the apprehension of mere contents without meaning or form. He has already done this by showing that content and form are inseparable; there is no mere sense content (sensation). Instead, all content is always already formed, always already infused with meaning. So the body does not apprehend mere content, because there is no mere content to be apprehended.

Second, Merleau-Ponty must show that the body is able not only to apprehend but also to bestow meaning, that there is a bestowal of meaning not only at the level of thought but also at the bodily level. That is precisely what the interrogation of sexuality seeks to accomplish.

Finally, Merleau-Ponty wants to show not only that the body is a locus of the emergence of meaning but also that it is the *primordial* locus. This requires showing that thought (and the kind of emergence of meaning at the level of thought) is in some way rooted in the emergence of meaning in the bodily dimension.

These three issues are of course those of the primacy of the sensible *logos* over the one of thought, the primacy of perception in its full sense: perception as originating, autonomous, and founding. It is primarily through an interrogation of language that Merleau-Ponty tries to establish the primacy of perception in the third sense. As regards sexuality and affectivity, the aim is to exhibit an *original* bodily bestowal of meaning.

* * *

Insofar as we tend to objectify things, we tend to regard meaning as there (in the things) and to lose sight of the subject's contribution. Hence Merleau-Ponty proposes to inquire into an area of our experience where the meaning involved is obviously only a meaning for us: "that sector of our experience which obviously has meaning and reality only for ourselves" (PP 154, 180).

The sector at issue is our "affective milieu" (PP 154, 180). So we will "try to see how a being or an object begins to exist for us through desire or love" (PP 154, 180).

Merleau-Ponty starts with the traditional conception of affective life and proceeds to the clinical example establishing that sexuality is neither a matter of physiology nor psychology, neither a matter of the objective body nor conscious thought. Thus, as always, it is necessary to introduce a third term between the traditional alternatives of thing and consciousness.

Merleau-Ponty's argument follows these lines:

In the traditional conception, affectivity is understood in terms of emotional states of pleasure and pain. These states are sealed within themselves (are nonintentional) and can be explained only in purely physiological terms (since the body is taken as a mechanical system). But it is obvious that our affective life is not totally independent of psychological factors. So the tradition allows that emotional life is "shot through with intelligence" (PP 154, 180). But this means only that representations can take the place of natural stimuli by way of association or conditioning. Consequently, there are only two factors involved: mere emotional states and representations. If this conception were correct, any sexual incapacity could be accounted for in terms of either a weakening of the capacity for satisfaction or a loss of certain representations.

In the case of Schneider, however, neither of these suffices to explain the deterioration of sexual life. There is a breakdown neither on the side of emotional states nor of representation. So there must be involved in sexuality another factor, one which is neither thing nor consciousness and which is operative in the normal subject but disrupted in the case of Schneider.

Merleau-Ponty identifies this factor as an erotic structure inherent in perceptual experience, as an "intentional arc" which, at a level prior to consciousness, endows things with sexual significance:

> There must be an eros or a libido animating an original world, giving sexual value or meaning to external stimuli, and predelineating the use subjects are to make of their objective body. It is this very structure of erotic perception or of erotic experience that has deteriorated in Schneider. For a normal subject, a body is not simply perceived like any other object; this objective perception is inhabited by a more secret one: the visible body is subtended by a strictly individual sexual schema. (PP 156, 182)

What is especially important is that this erotic structure, by which sexual significance is bestowed on a visible body, is not something projected by consciousness. Instead, a different kind of significance is involved, a bodily (not conceptual) significance—the new meaning of "meaning." What lies at the root of this significance is the *bodily* power of projecting a sexual world.

* * *

The remainder of the chapter is devoted to the problem of the relation between sexuality and conscious (personal) existence. In this discussion, Merleau-Ponty explicitly says he wants to retain what is of lasting value in psychoanalysis.

What Merleau-Ponty does is to restate with respect to sexuality what he has already established about the relation of bodily existence to conscious existence. There are two major points:

(1) Founding. We saw that the relation between the body and personal existence is a founding relation. This means the bodily level is taken up and transformed by personal existence. Yet, at the same time, the bodily dimension underlies, founds, is the necessary basis for, personal existence. (The body is that through which we are present to the world.) And this dimension is never totally left behind.

The same relation holds, then, between sexuality and personal existence. The latter takes up and transforms sexuality (desire becomes love), yet sexuality is never simply left behind, simply reduced to the personal level, any more than personal life is simply reducible to a sexual drama:

> Neither the body *nor personal existence* can be taken as the original moment of the human being, since each presupposes the other and since the body is congealed or generalized existence and existence is perpetual incarnation. In particular, when it is said that sexuality has an existential signification, or that it expresses existence, this must not be taken to mean that the sexual drama is in the last analysis *only* a manifestation or a symptom of an existential drama. The same reason preventing us from "reducing" existence to the body, or to sexuality, also prevents us from "reducing" sexuality to existence. (PP 166, 194)

(2) Ambiguity. Not only can we not reduce either to the other, we cannot even delimit once and for all the spheres of existence and sexuality sharply against each other. Each permeates the other in peculiar fashion:

> There is osmosis between sexuality and personal existence; if existence diffuses into sexuality, then, correlatively, so does sexuality diffuse into existence, with the result that it is impossible to assign, in a given decision or action, the portion of the motivation that is sexual and the portion of other motivations, impossible to characterize a decision or an act as "sexual" or "unsexual" *tout court*. Hence there reigns in human existence a principle of indeterminacy, and this indeterminacy does not exist only for us; it does not derive from some imperfection in our finite knowledge, and we must not believe that a God could sound our depths and delimit what in our existence comes from nature and what from freedom. Existence is in itself indeterminate, indeterminate in virtue of its fundamental structure, thus insofar as it is the very operation by which what had no meaning takes on meaning, by which what had merely sexual meaning takes on a more general signification, by which what is accidental is raised to the level of reason. In short, it is indeterminate insofar as existence is the appropriation of a factual situation. (PP 169, 197)

So Merleau-Ponty says that "ambiguity is of the essence of human existence" (PP 169, 197).

v. Part One of the *Phenomenology of Perception*:
Chapter 6. The Body as Expression; Speech

With respect to the thesis of the primacy of perception, the issue that remains to be worked out is that of the bodily bestowal of meaning as *primordial* for all other meaning. That thought is *rooted* in the bodily, perceptual domain represents a radical break with the tradition.

Thus far we have spoken as though the founding of judgment on perceptual experience is a self-evident starting point. But it must be established. The interrogation of language is a principal means by which Merleau-Ponty tries to establish it, and that is why language occupies such a central place in his phenomenology.

Let us begin by examining more precisely what Merleau-Ponty means by the primacy of perception. He says:

> What I want to express by this term is that the experience of perception puts us in the presence of the moment at which things, truths, and values are constituted for us, delivers up to us a *logos* in the nascent state, teaches us, outside of all dogmatism, the true conditions of objectivity itself, and recalls us to the tasks of knowledge and action. It is not at all a matter of reducing human knowledge to sensing, but of being in attendance at the birth of this knowledge, of rendering it as sensible as the sensible, of regaining the consciousness of rationality. (PR 25, 67)

In the essay from which this quotation derives, Merleau-Ponty makes specific reference to the death of God. With that death, we no longer have rationality, *logos*, truth, and value preserved and guaranteed by a metaphysical absolute and then somehow handed over to us. The only alternatives left are either a denial of *logos*, a denial which cannot even sustain itself and leads to skepticism, or the attempt to discover a *logos* on this side of all absolutes, to seek a *logos* born in experience itself and sustained by experience. Yet this latter *logos* cannot be a necessary eternal one; instead, it must be a *logos* bound to time and contingency, a "logic in contingency," an "incarnate logic" (S 88, 109).

The meaning of the primacy of perception is summarized even more clearly in this way: "The perceived world is the foundation always presupposed by all rationality, all value, and all existence. This thesis does not destroy either rationality or the absolute. It only tries to bring them down to earth" (PR 13, 43).

The primacy of perception with respect to thought involves three distinguishable aspects:

(1) The autonomy of perception as not rooted in thought.

(2) The rootedness (grounding) of thought in perception. The perceptual, bodily dimension is the fundamental stratum from which thought (the higher stratum) emerges without ever losing entirely its anchorage in the lower level.

(3) Consequently, there is an identity of structure as regards the two levels (perception-thought). The realm of thought, like that of perception, involves a certain openness. It is not a completed, self-contained intelligible world. It is open to further development. Moreover, the realm of thought involves the basic structure of sedimentation-spontaneity. Just like perception, it has a history which through sedimentation provides a springboard for further thought. That is, thought proceeds, not in a vacuum, but on the basis of what has already been accomplished by earlier thought.

So thought, like perception, has its roots in the past which is present to it by way of sedimentation, and it has an openness to the future. This means thought is not the entrance of the eternal into the temporal. Thought is subject to the fundamental structure of temporality just as is perception. "Thus perception and thought have this much in common: both of them have a future horizon and a past horizon and appear to themselves as temporal, even though they do not run their course at the same speed or in the same time" (PR 21, 58–59).

* * *

The goal of Merleau-Ponty's discussion of expression and speech is to exhibit the rootedness of thought in the perceptual-bodily dimension, the rootedness of the *logos* of thought in the *logos* of the sensible world. Merleau-Ponty assigns to speech a mediating role here: thought is bound up with speech, and in turn speech is rooted in perceptual life.

Let us outline his argument in eight steps:

(1) He begins with the traditional theories, namely, those of empiricism and intellectualism.

For empiricism, to know a language amounts to possessing certain mental traces that can be called up by appropriate stimuli. But that is obviously inadequate; in certain cases of aphasia it is clear that what is lost is not a stock of mental traces but rather a certain way of using words (such as in abstract situations). So there is some other factor (besides the mere stimulus) involved in speech—presumably thought. Thus we move to the position of intellectualism: what underlies speech is thought, specifically, the ability to subsume individual instances under a category.

(2) These two views are both unsatisfactory, for according to them the *word itself* has no meaning. The word is merely called up by something else (stimulus or thought). "Thus we transcend not only empiricism but also intellectualism by this simple observation: the word does *have* meaning" (PP 177, 206).

(3) For Merleau-Ponty, the word itself bears a meaning: there is a meaning "which is not simply *conveyed* by the words but which inhabits them and is inseparable from them" (PP 182, 212). Words are not mere external accompaniments of thought.

That is, in speaking we do not just translate ready-made thoughts. Instead, it is in speaking that thought is fulfilled, completed: "Thought tends toward expression as toward its completion" (PP 177, 206). That is why, according to Merleau-Ponty: "the most familiar thing appears indeterminate to us as long as we have not recalled its name, and the thinking subject is in a sort of ignorance of his own thoughts as long as he has not formulated them for himself" (PP 177, 206). Merleau-Ponty gives the following example: "The naming of objects is not subsequent to recognition; this naming is itself recognition. When I fix my gaze on an object in the half-light and finally say, 'It is a brush,' there is not in my mind a concept of brush, under which I would subsume the object and which had become joined, through frequent association, with the word 'brush.' On the contrary, the word itself bears the meaning, and by imposing the word on the object, I am conscious of attaining that object" (PP 177, 207).

So there is a kind of *thinking in speech*. This is evident when we ourselves speak or listen to someone else speaking. There is not, over and above the speaking or listening, an activity of conceptual thought for which words are merely signs. Instead, beneath whatever conceptual meaning I might later extract, there is layer of *existential meaning* in the words, a meaning which we live through and which forms the basis for subsequent conceptualizing.

(4) Thus thought is inextricably tied to speech. But, in turn, speech is something bodily, not only in the sense that bodily mechanisms are used in speaking, but also in a more basic sense.

Consider words themselves as they enter into one's speaking. When I speak, I do not first have to represent the word and then say it. Rather, the word enjoys a kind of potential presence. It is there as a possible use of my body: "I reach for a word the way my hand reaches for the place on my body that has been stung. The word is in a certain place in my linguistic world; it is part of my available capital" (PP 180, 210).

Thus speech is linked to the body. Yet this is not sufficient, for Merleau-Ponty wants to show not just this linkage, but that speech *originates* out of (is rooted in) being-in-the-world, the body's presence to the world.

(5) Thus the investigation must be pursued further. Recall that meaning inhabits words; there is not a "meaning thought" and a "word spoken." To that extent, speech is no different from gestures in the usual sense: a gesture (such as one of anger) is not something which *points* to a meaning; it *is* that meaning. Merleau-Ponty says, then, that speaking is a kind of gesture and like all gestures is situated in a certain common world which we share with others and which makes the gesture understandable.

What is this common world in the case of language? It is a world of available meanings, of already constituted and sedimented meanings left by former acts of expression. It is the world of meaning supported by a constituted language, a world available to me insofar as I am at home in the language. That is, the "word in the speaking" (*parole parlante*) always occurs against a background constituted by the "spoken word" (*parole parlée*).

(6) This inquiry points back to the origination of speech out of an already constituted language and the latter's world of meanings. But, this is not yet to see the origin of speech in being-in-the-world. What about the already constituted language? We are inclined to say that its relation to things is merely conventional, that language is not rooted in our presence to things but that words are made to designate things *by convention*.

Merleau-Ponty responds: human beings do not first of all make conventions and then begin to speak. So beneath the level of conventionality in language, there must be a core which is in some sense *natural*.

Yet language is not natural because of an objective resemblance to things. If we want to discover the natural core of language, we must go beneath the objective and conceptual level. We must take into account "the emotional content of the word." Then we would find "that words, vowels, and phonemes are so many ways of singing the world and that they serve to represent objects not, as the naive onomatopoeic theory believed, in virtue of an objective resemblance, but because they extract from objects their emotional essence and in the strict sense *express* that essence" (PP 187, 218).

Accordingly: "The predominance of vowels in one language, or of consonants in another, as well as the systems of construction and syntax, do not represent so many arbitrary conventions to express the same idea but, rather, various ways for the human body to celebrate the world and, ultimately, to live it. The result is that the *full* meaning of a language is never translatable into another" (PP 187, 218).

(7) So language and speech (and hence thought) have their roots in being-in-the-world, in a bodily presence to the world. And if the meaning of a sentence appears to be detachable from the sentence and from the existential basis of the meaning, if meanings can appear to constitute a self-subsistent intelligible domain (of pure thought), this is only because we take for granted and ignore the complex constitutive history behind language and meaning: "The apparent clarity of language rests on an obscure background" (PP 188, 219).

(8) Yet, finally, although speech has its roots in being-in-the-world and can never be totally uprooted, it does represent a *new level* of achievement: we cannot perceive our perception or paint about painting, but we can speak about speech.

* * *

In the end, what does Merleau-Ponty's philosophy of language accomplish?

Language, according to the usual view, signifies a preestablished domain of meaning. By signifying meaning, language has the capacity to refer to things insofar as they exemplify this meaning. But if that is so, then one could readily conclude that all languages are just imperfect approximations to an ideal language that would express fully the domain of preestablished meaning.

The immense diversity of languages already provokes doubt as to whether there is any such ideal language. And once the thesis that there is preestablished meaning is rejected, the entire structure supporting the thesis collapses.

Merleau-Ponty proceeds from this collapse in such a way as to avoid the conclusion that language is purely conventional. For Merleau-Ponty, meaning is not preestablished over and above our experience of things but instead is bound up in this experience. And language is joined to things because it is a way meaning is made to emerge.

But meaning can emerge in different ways because of the openness of the perceptual dimension (just as a thing can be seen from different perspectives). That is, there are radically different ways of inhabiting the world. They are irreducible to one another and cannot be subjected to and measured by some single, absolute, perfect, ideal way of inhabiting the world. From the standpoint of absolute thought, however, there is only one way of thinking the world. Hence, Merleau-Ponty allows for the real possibility of different languages, each with its own autonomy.

D. Part Two of the *Phenomenology of Perception*: The Perceived World

i. Introduction. The Theory of the Body Is Already a Theory of the Perceived World

Merleau-Ponty's retrieval of the phenomenal body has two major consequences. These are worked out in Parts Two and Three of the *Phenomenology of Perception*, respectively:

(1) If the body is subjectivized, then consciousness is, in turn, radically incarnated. That is, if consciousness is essentially founded on bodily existence and if that existence remains ever compromised by the body, then consciousness is never pure consciousness.

So there is no possibility of escaping entirely from being situated. As linked essentially to the body, consciousness is always cast into a situation: "But if our union with the body is a substantial one, how could we ever experience in ourselves a pure soul and from there accede to absolute Spirit?" (PP 199, 232).

What is thus called for is a reinterrogation of consciousness, of being-for-itself. That is the task of Part Three.

(2) To say that consciousness is never pure and cannot accede to absolute spirit is to say that we never cease to occupy a standpoint, can never regard things "from nowhere," can never take them as objects, as totally transparent. Instead, we can regard things only in reference to the way they are accessible to us through the body. The character of things cannot be determined independently of the way they show themselves through the body.

Merleau-Ponty's discussions have shown that the body is not an object of which we can form a clear and distinct idea. Once the body is subjectivized, it adheres to the subject and cannot be set at a distance (objectified and conceptualized as a third-person process). Rather, the body has an opaqueness, an obscurity for us: the bodily anchorage in the world is something already established which resists dissolution by analysis.

So, if things are linked to the body, this same opaqueness spreads to them— which is another way of saying we cannot regard them as objects: "The body does not stand out among all objects as being the only one to resist the grasp of pure reflection by remaining, as it were, too closely attached to the subject.

On the contrary, its obscurity encroaches on the perceived world as a whole" (PP 199, 232).

That expresses the problem of Part Two. The problem is summarized in the title of the introduction to this part. The title indicates that to know something of the body is already to know something of the things perceived by the body. Thus the theory of the body is already a theory of the perceived world.

Merleau-Ponty begins: "The body is in the world the way the heart is in the organism: it keeps the visible spectacle continuously alive, animates and nourishes it from within, and forms, together with that spectacle, a single system" (PP 203, 235).

We can use some of the concrete descriptions we developed previously to see what Merleau-Ponty means by saying that the body and the world form a system.

Consider perceptual experience. Given in that domain are only profiles. Yet the thing itself is not just a profile or a series of profiles. Instead, the thing is beyond all profiles. It is what is seen from nowhere or from everywhere. The problem is how it happens that our experience is an experience of things, not just of profiles. How does it happen that our experience reaches beyond profiles to the thing itself?

One way (the intellectualistic way) of accounting for this is to maintain that the thing itself is something *conceived* (since it is not given) when I *interpret* perceptual appearances and, so to speak, discount the distortion my bodily position introduces into these appearances (for example, in perceiving a cube). Merleau-Ponty raises two objections against this account:

(1) I do not in fact need to acquire an objective view of my bodily position and movement and subsequently take that view into account in order to reconstruct the thing itself. I do not, as a rule, have any such objective view at all. Furthermore, I do not take my body explicitly into account. Instead, "the account is already taken" in perception itself but not by way of subtracting the distorting effect of my body. Rather, my body is integrated into the perceptual act; and it is precisely in this system (body-appearances) that the thing itself appears: "External perception and the perception of one's own body therefore vary together, since they are the two faces of one and the same act" (PP 205, 237).

(2) Second, the thing is not conceived by inference *beyond* the profiles. Instead, the thing is already there in the profiles, already reveals itself through the profiles. The unity of the thing is not a mere conceptual unity but is one standing out through the profiles and correlative to the unity of my body.

Thus the phenomenal body and the perceived world form a system. We do not have the object on one side and, on the other, a bodily subject with its merely subjective appearances, from which to reach the object by inference. Instead, the profiles reveal the things, open onto the world, and through the profiles the bodily subject is, from the outset, open to the world and with it forms a single system.

Consequently, since body and world form a system, it follows that if the body displays certain structures (ones unintelligible to objective thought), these structures "will be passed on to the sensible world." In other terms, if we withdraw the body from the domain of objectivity, it will drag along with it the objects to which it is intentionally connected.

Hence the task of Part Two: "We now need to reawaken the experience of the world as it appears to us insofar as we are involved in the world by means of our body and insofar as we perceive the world with our body" (PP 206, 239).

ii. Part Two of the *Phenomenology of Perception*:
Chapter 1. Sense Experience

Let us examine this chapter by taking up in succession its six main themes.

(1) Return to the incarnate subject.

Empiricism theorizes a ready-made (objective) world and treats perception as just another causal event in this world. Thus empiricism completely immerses the subject in the world and does incarnate the subject but overlooks its character as a subject.

The empiricist can overlook this character only because he forgets himself. More specifically, he overlooks the fact that it is through perception that there is a world present to us in the first place and that all knowledge takes place in the horizon opened up by perception. In other words, a picture of the world necessarily excludes the point from which the picturing takes place: "It would be out of the question to describe perception itself as one of the facts occurring in the world, since it is impossible to eliminate from the picture of the world that lacuna which we ourselves are and by which the world comes to exist for us at all—in other words, since perception is a 'flaw' in this 'great diamond.'" (PP 207, 240).

Intellectualism follows up such criticism by turning this outside point of view into a transcendental ego, an absolute constituting consciousness of which the world is the mere correlate. But that position goes too far; it completely excludes the subject from the world. Intellectualism does retain the character of the subject as subject but denies its incarnation.

Because intellectualism places the subject totally outside the world, insurmountable difficulties arise. Intellectualism cannot explain the limitations and ambiguity in our knowledge of the world. If consciousness simply constitutes its object, there would be no separation between itself and its object, and so things could not present themselves as inexhaustible. In other words, intellectualism cannot answer the question: "How does it come about that we perceive?"

The difficulty results from the basic affinity of intellectualism with empiricism, namely, its retaining the ready-made world of empiricism and simply making it the correlate of consciousness. A ready-made world requires that the subject be either completely inside or completely outside that world. Merleau-Ponty proposes to avoid both total inclusion and total exclusion. That is, he proposes to show that we can never fully become a transcendental ego: every personal act retains a background of pre-personal life through which we remain immersed in the world and never escape from that world.

For Merleau-Ponty the subject is both immersed in the world (and thus is incarnate and finite) and yet transcends the world (thus is genuinely a subject). The subject must be an incarnate subject and exemplify finite transcendence.

If the world is to admit this ambivalent presence of the subject, then the world cannot be regarded as fully determinate and ready-made, thereby totally excluding or totally including the subject. Instead, Merleau-Ponty proposes to delve beneath the level at which we have a ready-made subject either inside or outside a ready-made world, to return to the ambivalent presence of the subject to the world at a level where each is continually in the making:

> We have the experience of a world, not in the sense of a system of relations which are entirely determinative of every event, but as an open totality, whose synthesis can never be completed. We have the experience of an ego, not in the sense of an absolute subjectivity, but as constantly unmade and remade in the course of time. The unity of the subject, like the unity of the object, is not an actually instituted unity but is a presumptive unity on the horizon of experience, and we must rediscover, on this side of the *ideas* of subject and object, the *facticity* of my subjectivity and the object *in its nascent state*. That is, we must rediscover the primordial stratum where ideas as well as things are born. (PP 219, 254)

(2) Immersion of the subject in perception.

Merleau-Ponty wants to show that the subject is not a detached observer aloof from the world (a for-itself over against an in-itself) but rather that the subject is drawn into the world. In sense experience the subject is genuinely immersed in the world and forms a system with it.

So Merleau-Ponty takes up again the problem of sensation and extends his critique of the idea of sensation. He refers to the fact that sensations (for example, colors) have an inherent motor meaning; colors provoke incipient movements. This entails that the very reception of sensations already involves a response by the subject. It is not as though sensations are first given and then there is a response. Rather, sense experience is holistic, and within it the given and the response are inseparable moments. If the response by the subject is required for there even to be sense experience, then the subject cannot simply "stand back" and observe what is given, cannot simply be for-itself.

Let us look at this issue in a slightly different way. The relation of the perceptual subject to the perceived is a dialogue; there is a contribution on both sides. I must adopt an appropriate bodily attitude, although this attitude alone is insufficient. I must also be plunged into the sensible; it must open up and give itself to me:

> The sensing subject and the sensible do not face each other in the manner of two mutually external terms, and sensation is not an invasion of that subject by the sensible. Color itself depends on my gaze, the very form of the object depends on the movement of my hand, or, rather, my gaze and the color are wedded so intimately, just as are my hand and hardness or softness, that in the interchange between the sensing subject and the sensible it is impossible to specify which one is acting and which one is undergoing the action, which one is giving meaning and which one is receiving it. Unless my gaze or my hand explores it, and before my body synchronizes with it, the sensible is nothing but a vague solicitation. (PP 214, 247–48)

So the perceptual subject cannot remain outside the world, a mere for-itself, but rather is drawn into and immersed in the world, involved in a dialogue with the world. Indeed, the subject is to a degree something for-itself (it is consciousness, a subject, not a thing). But it is a for-itself which is "saturated with its objects," immersed in the world, hence never completely for-itself (contra Sartre).

This has two consequences.

First, perceptual consciousness is not completely self-transparent, not pure self-consciousness, not pure presence of itself to itself. It never has itself totally in its grasp. That is what Merleau-Ponty means by saying perception is anonymous, general, something *one* does, not something *I* do. Perception is beneath the level of personal existence:

> By way of sensation, I grasp, on the margin of my personal life, on the margin of my acts in the proper sense, a given life of consciousness from which these acts emerge; this prior life is the one of my eyes, of my hands, of my ears, which are so many natural egos. Every time I experience a sensation, I recognize that it does not pertain to my own being, the one for which I am responsible and about which I make decisions, but to another ego that has already decided in favor of the world, that has already opened itself to certain aspects of the world, and that is already synchronized with them. Between my sensation and me there is always the thickness of an *originary acquisition*, which prevents my experience from ever being clear to itself. (PP 216, 250)

The second consequence is that perception is always partial, incomplete. I am subject to a certain field. I am not like an absolute observer who, completely outside the world, could hold it all in view. Instead, I have no such distance. I am immersed in the world and perceive it from this position within it. Hence I never perceive it exhaustively:

We can summarize by saying that every sensation belongs to a certain *field*. That I have a visual field means that I am open to a system of beings—visual beings—and have access to them: they are available to my gaze in virtue of a kind of primordial contract and through a gift of nature, without any effort on my part. To say that I have a visual field thus means that vision is pre-personal, and at the same time it means that vision is always limited, that around my present vision there is always a horizon of things not yet seen or not even visible at all. (PP 216, 250–51)

(3) The spatiality of the senses.

In order to penetrate further into our perceptual involvement with the world, Merleau-Ponty now takes up the question of the relation between various senses and the relation of the senses to the experience of space. How are the various senses related to space?

All the senses are spatial insofar as they open onto a world. Even the simplest sensation presents a figure *standing out* in front of a ground and hence is spatial. But do all the senses simply open onto one and the same space? In other words, is there simply one space which all the senses disclose?

Indeed, Kant showed that such a single space is necessary—*for objectivity*. But it is precisely such a completed and objective world that Merleau-Ponty does not want to assume. Instead, he wants to go back to the origin of that space in our sense experience. He wants to take what Kant considered necessary (and which may be necessary at the level of objective thought) and trace it back to our pre-personal, perceptual contact with the world.

Merleau-Ponty begins by noting that each sense presents a differently structured space. This is evident in the case of blind persons who gain their sight after an operation. They marvel at visual space; it is so different from the space previously accessible to them that they feel they have never really experienced space before.

But space is not merely visual. All the senses are spatial: "Each sense organ interrogates objects in its own way and is the agent of a specific type of synthesis" (PP 223, 258). On the other hand, there is a unity among these spaces. The unity rests on the fact that there is *communication* among the senses, as we see by the special effort necessary to focus on a single sense.

In other words, prior to any division among the senses, we find a "primary layer" of sense experience in which all the senses interpenetrate. This is evident in the cases of synaesthetic experience (for instance, under mescaline one can literally see a sound and hear a color).

Merleau-Ponty proceeds to specify what is involved in the communication of the senses. They communicate because they open onto the same thing, manifesting its same structure in different ways: "The senses communicate among themselves by opening out onto the structure of the thing. We see the rigidity and fragility of glass, and when it breaks with a crystalline sound, even this sound is borne by the visible glass. We see the ductility of the red-hot ingot, the resilience of the finished steel, the hardness of the blade of a carpenter's plane, the softness of the shavings" (PP 229, 265).

This suggests that the unity of the thing is the ground of the unity among the senses, the ground of their intercommunication. But it is not so simple. For how is the unity of a thing to be accounted for? It is not something posited independently of sense experience but, instead, is constituted only in and through that experience. This is not a matter of one unity being prior to the other; instead, it is a matter of coordinating unities, communicating unites. In other words, the subject and the perceived form a whole, a system.

The task is then to interrogate more closely this whole, this system of subject-world, and to engage in a reflection which is appropriate. Such a reflection would not dissolve this whole into a subject side and a separate object side but would rather in some way bring to light the articulations of this whole itself, this primordial linking (gearing, meshing) of the subject to things. Such reflection will also illuminate the other features: perception as a locus of meaning and the relation of the subject with things.

Let us try to specify the problem more precisely.

Again we take our departure from our concrete descriptions. Only profiles are directly presented, but our experience is an experience of things themselves. How does the subject transcend the profiles so as to intend the thing itself? We suggested that horizon-structures are involved in some way here. But let us see more closely how so.

The thing is not intended independently of the profiles and is not inferred behind them. Instead, the thing is aimed at *through* the profiles. That means it is through a synthesis of the various profiles that the thing is intended. But that is possible only if the profiles are somehow in view, hence the importance of the inner horizon.

So the thing is the synthetic unity inherent in the profiles. Then we can formulate more precisely the problem of the linking of the subject to things: it is a problem of synthesis. The central problem on which Merleau-Ponty's efforts thus converge is the nature of this synthesis.

In the chapter on "Sense Experience," three features of this synthesis are brought to light: the perceptual synthesis is bodily, anonymous, and temporal. The character of the synthesis is then greatly elaborated in Chapters 2 and 3 on space and on the thing and the natural world.

(4) Perceptual synthesis as bodily.

We saw that the subject sustains a world of things only in relation to the way it is addressed by things. That means the synthesis by which the thing is constituted does not take place in a different dimension from that in which we are addressed by the thing. Instead, the synthesis occurs in the very midst of our being addressed. That is to say, the synthesis is not performed by conscious thought; it is instead a bodily synthesis. The body is the agent of this synthesis.

Merleau-Ponty explains how the unity of the object is constituted by drawing an analogy with what happens in the passage from double vision to the vision of a single thing. Here we have neither an inspection by the mind nor a purely physiological mechanism. Rather, the double object poses a problem, invites my gaze, and collapses into a single object when my eyes take up this invitation, when I use my eyes in a certain way so that I can plunge into the perceptual field:

> The two images of diplopia are not *physically* fused into a single image in binocular vision; on the contrary, the unity of the object is very much an intentional unity. For all that, however, it is not a conceptual unity. That is the point we wanted to establish. The passage from diplopia to the unitary object is not due to a mental inspection; it takes place when the two eyes cease to function each on its own account and are wielded as a single organ by a unitary gaze. It is not the epistemological subject that effects this synthesis; it is the body— when it snatches itself from dispersion, collects itself, and bears itself by all its means toward one single goal of its movement, that is, when, in virtue of the phenomenon of synergy, a unitary intention is born in it. (PP 232, 268–69)

So, more generally, what is involved is a *bodily* synthesis (a synthesis carried out by the body, not by thought) that constitutes the unity of the thing. Yet this synthesis is not accomplished in complete indifference to the way things address us; on the contrary, it is something prompted by the things.

(5) Perceptual synthesis as anonymous.

The synthesis of the perceptual object is situated in perception itself; it is a bodily synthesis. Now, the bodily dimension is anonymous. This means that a bodily synthesis is not something I simply initiate and carry through in the manner of a deliberate decision; rather, it is something always already under way, flowing on beneath the level of personal existence: "My act of naive perception is not itself that which effectuates this synthesis. My perception profits from work already accomplished, profits from a general synthesis constituted once and for all, which is what I express by saying that I perceive *with* my body or *with* my senses, for my body and my senses are precisely this habitual knowledge of the world, this implicit or sedimented science" (PP 238, 275).

The perceptual synthesis, as anonymous, makes use of something it takes for granted: "If, as we said, all perception has something anonymous about it, that is because it appropriates an acquisition it never places in question" (PP 238, 275).

What Merleau-Ponty means is that the perceptual synthesis takes place within an already established system in which the body is already anchored in the world, geared into the world. This system is one in which there are structures already constituted, thus a system in which the products of previous syntheses are established and retained as sedimented and which constitute a "primal acquisition" pointing back into an obscure past: "In perception we do not think the object, and we do not think ourselves thinking it; on the contrary, we are given over to the object and we merge into this body which knows more than we do about the world, about the motives and means we have to synthesize it" (PP 238, 275–76).

It is because these structures are already there that a synthesis is always already under way and hence does not have to begin "from scratch" with each new thing perceived. Merleau-Ponty says: "The one who perceives is not arrayed before himself, as a consciousness ought to be; the perceiver has historical thickness, he appropriates a perceptual tradition and is confronted with something present" (PP 238, 275).

(6) Perceptual synthesis as temporal.

This synthesis is temporal in a dual sense. First, the synthesis of the thing is based on the unfolding of time, on that primordial synthesis of past, present, and future which is the unfolding of time. We can see this by analogy with the focusing of the eyes: the final form of the thing (as it will appear in clear focus) is anticipated at the inception of the act of focusing, and as anticipated it is retained throughout the process. According to Merleau-Ponty, "The synthesis of space and the synthesis of the object are founded on this unfolding of time. In every movement of focusing, my body binds together a present, a past, and a future." (PP 239, 277)

Second, the perceptual synthesis is rooted in the past, not only in the sense of immediate retention, but also in that it presupposes a perceptual history, which places at my disposal an opaque acquisition. Perception retains the past in the depth of the present; it makes use of what is already constituted.

The whole problem of temporality is only broached here, and the full discussion is reserved for the second chapter of Part Three. But Merleau-Ponty does want to point to the fact that his whole problematic, in a sense, converges on the problem of temporality: "The perceptual synthesis is for us a temporal synthesis; subjectivity, at the level of perception, is nothing other than temporality, which is what allows us to do justice to the opacity and historicity of the perceiving subject" (PP 239, 276).

Subjectivity *is* temporality and as such has an opacity and a historicity; in other words, the subject is nonabsolute. Merleau-Ponty's central problem of accounting for a nonabsolute subject, for "finite subjectivity," carries him back, in the end, to the problem of temporality.

* * *

Merleau-Ponty has proposed to undo the objectification accomplished by science. It is an objectification into which we are "lured" by things and is the result of our natural propensity to lose ourselves in the things experienced and over-look experience itself.

The *Phenomenology of Perception* marks a radical break with this natural tendency and attempts to reverse it and undo what it has accomplished. So Merleau-Ponty wants to turn back to experience, that is, to a dimension prior to the one of objectivity. It is in this prior dimension that we first have access to things. It is the dimension presupposed by objective thought and of which such thought is a mere second-order expression. It is the dimension of perceptual experience.

The return was proposed in the Preface and the Introduction of the *Phenomenology of Perception*. In our considerations of Part One and the first chapter of Part Two, we have seen how Merleau-Ponty executes this return. Specifically, we have seen various features of this pre-objective dimension brought to light. Exactly how they are brought to light—what kind of reflection is being carried out—remains a problem. But it is a difficult problem to pose in an appropriate way, and we should perhaps let it remain a problem for a while yet.

At this point I want to draw together the various issues we have pursued and consolidate those features of the perceptual dimension Merleau-Ponty has brought out thus far. Thereby we will be in a better position to pose the major issue we are about to take up and will have a basis for a transition to the extremely crucial third part of the *Phenomenology of Perception*.

So let us consider the principal features of the perceptual dimension:

(1) Things are not objects.

That is, things as perceived cannot be equated with objects in the scientific sense. In distinction to objects, things as perceived involve gaps, ambiguity, inde-terminacy, and a dependence on context. For example, a cube as perceived is not a cube as understood objectively, scientifically.

(2) The subject is not an object.

That is, the subject cannot be regarded as a thing in the objective sense, as an objective body conceived as the seat of various causal processes. Instead, Merleau-Ponty (especially in *The Structure of Behavior*) has withdrawn the body from the objective world and has retrieved the phenomenal (subjectivized) body.

(3) The subject is not pure consciousness.

That is, the subject cannot be regarded as a transcendental subject aloof from the world but is rather always already in the world (being-in-the-world). The subject does not simply constitute the world, for instance by imposing form on a formless, meaningless sense-material. On the contrary, the subject sustains a world of things only in relation to the way it is addressed by those things.

(4) The perceptual subject is not the personal, conscious subject.

That is, the perceptual subject is not transparent to itself; it has a kind of anonymity. It is pre-personal and flows on beneath the level of personal life. The latter is founded on it and compromised by it.

(5) The perceptual subject is a bodily subject.

That is, the subject as bodily has "already sided" with the world, since the body is the vehicle of our inherence in the world. Thus Merleau-Ponty has replaced the traditional dualism of consciousness and body by a new dualism of two levels within subjectivity. But the boundary separating the two levels remains fluid. So this is a relative dualism.

(6) The perceptual domain is a locus of the emergence of meaning.

That is, in our bodily inherence in the world we are always already engaged with meaning. Meaning does not first arise through a meaning-bestowal by an act of conscious thought. Accordingly, there is a *logos* of the sensible world, as Merleau-Ponty showed in his study of sexuality.

(7) The perceptual dimension is the primordial locus of meaning. That is, thought in some way has its roots in (is founded on) perception. The *logos* of the sensible world has primacy over the *logos* of thought. Merleau-Ponty tried to show this (although only in a preliminary way) in the discussion of language.

(8) The subject and the world form a system, a whole.

That is, they are linked together, and not like two things that first exist in isolation and subsequently are connected up. Rather, each is what it is only in being bound to the other, and analysis cannot simply dissolve this relation. The perceptual dimension is one of an ambivalent presence of the subject to the world.

iii. Part Two of the *Phenomenology of Perception*: Chapter 2. Space

We reviewed various features Merleau-Ponty has brought to light in the primordial, pre-objective dimension of perceptual experience. We saw that all these features converge in Merleau-Ponty's thesis that the perceptual subject and the world form a system. We tried to articulate the problem involved in interrogating this system and posed it as a problem of *synthesis*.

The task is then to bring to light that synthesis by which the subject and the world form a system, that is to say, by which the subject transcends the immediately given (the profile) so as to intend things.

We gained an initial characterization of this synthesis. First, it is bodily, and that means the body—not consciousness—is the agent of the synthesis. It also means the synthesis takes place in dialogue with things, in relation to the way the bodily subject is addressed by things. Second, the synthesis is anonymous. It is not something I simply initiate and carry through; instead, it flows on beneath the level of personal existence, within an already established bodily anchorage in the world.

The problem of space is part of this more general problem of synthesis. The specific problem concerns how space is involved in the whole formed by the subject and the world.

We can best understand Merleau-Ponty's problem by contrasting it with the Kantian concept of space. For Kant, space is a form (of intuition) distinct from the content of experience. Also, space has its origin in consciousness, indeed not in thought but in pure intuition. Space is a form the mind gives to itself.

Merleau-Ponty wants to return from objective space (such as that of Kant) to the lived space of perceptual experience and to show that, just as with synthesis in general, space is not a mere form distinct from content or, in other words, is not constituted independently of the way things address us. Space is constituted not by consciousness but by the body.

Merleau-Ponty will show that spatial meanings (such as "up" and "down") originate in the perceptual-bodily dimension. Thereby he will again show that this dimension is the locus of an emergence of meaning. Furthermore, since spatial meanings are so omnipresent at the level of language and thought, he will contribute further to demonstrating the primacy of perception.

a.) Spatial directionality.

Consider the lived experience of "top" and "bottom." How can one account for the presence of such spatial meanings in the perceptual field?

Objective thought (empiricism or intellectualism) is oblivious to this problem, since, in objective space, there is no "up" or "down."

Merleau-Ponty cites two experimental situations involving spatial directionality, cases objective thought is entirely incapable of comprehending. The cases are vision without the ordinary retinal inversion and vision in which everything is tilted 45 degrees. Under these conditions, spatial directionality disintegrates and is then reconstituted.

Consider the traditional accounts. Empiricism tries to understand the emergence of directionality in terms of sense-content. Content, however, as understood by empiricism has no direction, no orientation. Intellectualism goes to the opposite extreme: space is a matter, not of content, but of a form bestowed by the subject. Space is a system of relations established by the unifying activity of consciousness.

But mere objective relations, no matter their origin, cannot provide any spatial directionality. For, directionality requires a preferred system of coordinates (vertical and horizontal). But objective relations of the sort instituted by constituting consciousness are invariant with respect to all coordinate systems and hence cannot supply any system as preferred.

Thus objective thought could not distinguish between an inverted world and the world right side up. The terms "inverted" and "right side up" do not even make any sense in such thought. If there is to be directionality, there must be a preferred coordinate system, an "absolute here." That is, the subject must be in the world in such a way as to establish through his presence certain lines of directionality.

Thus directionality is unintelligible if the subject is totally immersed in the world (merely receptive of content) and also if the subject is a constituting consciousness totally outside of the world. Again we see Merleau-Ponty's alternative: the subject must be both in the world and outside the world, thus in the world *as* subject.

Let us consider Merleau-Ponty's account of the experiment of seeing everything in a mirror which tilts the visual spectacle 45 degrees. At the beginning there is a certain "spatial level" or coordinate system in relation to which the new spectacle appears oblique. In the course of the experiment, this spectacle induces another spatial level in relation to which the spectacle appears straight and no longer oblique: "It is as if certain objects . . . appearing to be tilted in relation to the already given spatial level, claim for themselves the right to furnish the privileged directions, inasmuch as these objects attract the vertical to themselves, play the role of 'anchoring points,' and reorient the previously established spatial level" (PP 249, 287–88).

Such a process can be understood only in terms of a certain gearing of the body to the world. That is to say, against the background of its previous spatial level, the body is able to induce another level which makes it possible for the body to be "at home" in the world, to inhabit it.

Accordingly, the new spatial level is not inferred from sense-contents, nor is it simply created and imposed on the world by an aloof subject. Instead, it is instituted by the bodily subject in relation to and through its directedness toward the world, its engagement in the world. "Thus the spatial level is a certain possession of the world by my body, a certain *purchase* of my body on the world" (PP 250, 289). That is why the process seems to take pace *in* the world, why certain objects assume the role of "anchoring points."

More specifically, the process of restoring upright directionality while viewing the world through the mirror involves these stages:

(1) There is an already established spatial level (directionality) in relation to which the spectacle appears oblique.

(2) The bodily subject is disoriented in relation to this spectacle, not at home in this environment.

(3) Having been thus addressed by things, the bodily subject then establishes another level making it possible for the body to be at home in the world, to inhabit the world:

> After not many minutes, as long as the subject does not reinforce his original anchorage by casting his gaze outside of the mirror, this marvel occurs: the reflected room summons up a subject capable of living in it. This virtual body displaces the real body, so much so that the subject no longer feels himself in the world in which he is located objectively, and he feels, instead of his de facto arms and legs, the arms and legs he needs in order to walk and act in the reflected

room. In short, he comes to inhabit the spectacle. At the same moment, the spatial level tilts and establishes itself in a new position. (PP 250, 289)

(4) Yet this establishing of a new level is accomplished only as prompted by the way the things address the subject. That is why the process seems to take place *in* the world. Certain things act as "anchoring points" and attract the vertical axis to themselves.

Thus, spatial directionality is constituted not by consciousness but by the bodily subject. Furthermore, this directionality is not a mere form independent of content; it is not established independently of the way the subject is addressed by the things.

* * *

It is essential to note precisely what Merleau-Ponty has accounted for, namely, not how directionality first comes to be present in the world but instead, how, when one spatial level is disrupted, another is constituted against that background. This implies that the constitution of any spatial level always presupposes another previously established level. Space always precedes itself, is always already constituted.

Therefore, we can never isolate a pure nonspatial subject and object so as to ask how they come to be involved with space. Rather, they are always already spatial. The question of why subject and object are spatial is phenomenologically unintelligible, which is what Merleau-Ponty means by saying that space is "impenetrable to reflection" (PP 254, 294). Accordingly, he says:

> It is essential to space to be always "already constituted," and we will never comprehend space if we withdraw into a perception without a world. The task is not to question why being is oriented. . . . Such a question could be posed only if the facts expressed an accident befalling a subject and an object that are indifferent to space. Quite to the contrary, however, perceptual experience shows that the facts are presupposed in our primordial encounter with being and that to be and to be oriented are synonymous. For the thinking subject, a face seen "right side up" and the same face seen "upside down" are equivalent. But for the perceiving subject, the face seen "upside down" is unrecognizable. (PP 252, 291–92)

Thus the orientation of an object in space is not some contingent character superadded to it. Instead, its being-oriented is an essential element of its being as such: "To turn an object upside down is to take away its meaning. Its being as an object is therefore not a being-for-the-thinking-subject but is, instead, a being-for-the-gaze which encounters it under a certain visual angle and otherwise does not at all recognize it" (PP 253, 292).

Its being is a being for a perceptual subject. Likewise for the subject: the subject is always already geared to a spatial level. We could ask how it first comes to be geared only if we supposed that the subject was first of all worldless and then subsequently came to have a world. But the subject is being-in-the-world.

All that one can do is to point back to one's pre-personal pact with the world and acknowledge, as Merleau-Ponty says, that "My history is the resumption of a prehistory, a resumption that uses the results of this pre-history as an acquisition, and my personal existence is the appropriation of a pre-personal tradition" (PP 254, 293).

b.) Depth.

Traditional analyses deny that depth is really visible, and so they conclude that the appearance of depth results from an inference or from some other activity on the part of the subject.

Indeed, depth is not visible if it is simply equated with breadth seen end-on. But is this equating so obvious when we situate ourselves within perception? Does it not already assume a uniform, isotropic space—space not as it is given to the finite perceptual subject but rather a space that could appear only to a ubiquitous subject, one who is or presumes to be everywhere and nowhere?

According to Merleau-Ponty, these accounts "assume as self-evident the result of a constitutive operation whose phases we ourselves, on the contrary, must trace out. In order to treat depth as breadth viewed end-on, to arrive at isotropic space, the subject must leave his place, his point of view on the world, and think himself into a sort of ubiquity. For God, who is everywhere, breadth is immediately equivalent to depth. Intellectualism and empiricism do not give us an account of the human experience of the world; what they tell us about the world is merely what God would think of it" (PP 255, 295–96).

This equating may be established and believed within the already constituted, intersubjective, public world. But Merleau-Ponty's aim is to return—beneath this—to perceptual life.

In the traditional views, the experience of depth has generally been explained as resulting from the *interpretation* of certain given conditions of the objective body: the convergence of the eyes, the size of the retinal images, the accommodation of the lenses, and so on. Merleau-Ponty raises these objections:

(1) Such an interpretation would require that we have already placed our eyes and the object in objective space. How otherwise could we interpret the convergence of the eyes as a sign of depth?

But it is precisely this objective space that we cannot presuppose, since our aim is to go back to a level prior to its emergence: "Since perception is our very initiation into the world . . . we may not attribute to perception objective relations that are not yet constituted at its level" (PP 257, 297).

(2) In perceiving depth, I am not aware of these "conditions." I am unaware of the convergence of my eyes and the size of the visual image. That image has no

measurable size in normal perception. So there are simply no perceived conditions on which I could base an interpretation.

In response to these objections, it might be maintained that, rather than being the basis for an interpretation, these factual occurrences are the *causes* of depth perception. Again, Merleau-Ponty objects:

(1) This causality is not supported by experimentation; there is no exact correlation between the size of the visual image and depth perception.

(2) Such an explanation again retreats into objectivity, which is constituted only from out of the perceptual order.

Thus Merleau-Ponty concludes that all these factors represent various interrelated phases of our comprehensive organization of the visual field. One is not the cause of the other; instead, they are related in the manner of motive and decision: "The motive is an antecedent acting solely in virtue of its meaning; moreover, the decision is what confirms this meaning as a valid one and gives the motive its force and efficacy" (PP 259, 299). So likewise as regards "apparent size" and depth:

> The relation between the motivating and the motivated is thus a reciprocal one. Now such is indeed the relation that exists between the experience of convergence, or of apparent size, and the experience of depth. The convergence and apparent size do not, in the guise of 'causes,' miraculously make appear an organization in depth; on the contrary, they tacitly motivate this organization inasmuch as they already enclose it in their own meaning and inasmuch as both these factors are already a certain manner of gazing into the distance. (PP 259, 299–300)

Yet why do we tend to conceive depth perception as a matter of interpretation? Primarily because of perspective drawings in which we perceive a depth which is not really there. But, rather than supporting this theory of interpretation, perspective drawings illustrate the genuine character of depth perception. In perceiving the drawing, there is not first a positing of a flat configuration of lines and then an interpretation. Instead, under our gaze the drawing itself strives for equilibrium by delving into depth: "The totality of the drawing seeks its equilibrium by organizing itself according to depth and becoming concave. The roadside poplar, drawn smaller than a man, succeeds in decisively becoming a tree only by receding toward the horizon. The drawing itself tends toward depth just as a falling stone tends toward what is down below" (PP 262, 303).

We see then to what extent depth perception is rooted in the dialogue between the body and the world, in the directedness, engagement, involvement of the subject in the world.

c.) Motion.

Here, too, Merleau-Ponty wants to get back beneath objectivity, beneath the objective idea of movement, and uncover the pre-objective experience in which movement first comes to exist for us. He wants to return to that level at which the experience of movement is still bound up with the subject's fundamental anchorage in the world.

This return is especially difficult, for in the case of movement we tend immediately to adopt an artificial attitude. Suppose I throw a stone. It remains the same throughout, unmodified by the movement. Movement is a mere accidental attribute of a moving body, a mere change in the relations between the stone and its surroundings. Thus movement is not seen "in the stone." All we have is a change in the relations between the stone and some landmark. There is then no absolute movement, no movement without some landmark.

Thus we distinguish rigorously between movement and the object which moves. That object does not really *undergo* movement; instead, movement is a mere change in external relations: "To distinguish rigorously between motion and the moving object is to say that, in the strict sense, the 'moving object' *does not move*" (PP 268, 310).

The objective account, however, is not borne out if we go back to our perception of movement. I perceive movement without perceiving an identical moving object at each point along the course of motion. Nor do I explicitly refer the movement to some frame of reference. Instead, the movements I see present themselves as absolute.

We need to understand these features:

(1) There is continuity and unity in movement. But this is not a unity grasped separately from ("beneath") the movement, not a unity grasped through a synthesis of static points:

> The moving object, or, rather, as we said, the moving something-or-other, is not identical *beneath* the phases of the motion, it is identical *in* them. It is not *because* I find the same stone on the ground that I believe in its identity in the course of its motion. On the contrary, it is because I perceived it as identical in the course of its motion—in the form of an implicit identity which remains to be described—that I go over to it and do find it. We should not attribute to the stone-in-motion everything we otherwise know about the stone. (PP 273, 316)

The identity, the unity, is a unity on this side of objectivity. It is not a unity of explicit perceptions but a unity of style, a *lived* unity:

> For example, at the very moment of its motion, the bird flying across my garden is no more than a certain grayish power of flight. More generally, as we will see, things define themselves primarily by their "behavior" and not by their static "properties." It is not that I recognize, at each of the traversed points and instants, the same bird defined by explicit characteristics; on the contrary, the flying bird itself brings about the unity of its motion, the bird itself displaces itself, and this feathery tumult itself, which is still here, is already over there in a sort of ubiquity, like a comet with its tail. (PP 275, 318)

(2) Movement is always movement within a setting. But this is not to make movement merely relative. If movement were so, then all settings would be interchangeable. But that is not the case. In the concrete act of perceiving movement, the movement is perceived *as* absolute, and the setting is *the* one appropriate for viewing this movement.

How does a particular setting emerge as preferred so as to give our perception of its movement an absolute character? It does so precisely insofar as the human body provides itself with certain anchoring points in the world. There is a natural setting for movement *through* the body's engagement, anchorage, in the world: "The human body furnishes the perception of movement the ground on which this perception must be established, and the body does so insofar as it is a perceiving power, insofar as it itself is already established in a certain domain and geared into a world" (PP 279, 323).

d.) Spatiality.

In all three areas investigated (directionality, depth, and movement), we have been led back to the fundamental inherence of the subject in the world, the subject's anchorage in the world. We have seen that in each case it is not a matter of something posited by the subject. For example, directionality is always already established by our body, not posited by consciousness. As regards the perception of movement, we do not have a fully determinate, posited object that moves. Instead, we perceive something incomplete and implicit, a style that we recognize: "We hardly perceive any *objects*, just as we do not see the eyes of a familiar face but only its mien or expression. There is a latent meaning, one that, without needing to be explicitly defined, presents itself in its own specific evidence" (PP 281, 325).

Things are not posited by the subject; instead, our perception is *borne along* by our inherence in the world, our anchorage in it, our gearing into it. Therefore, we must recognize a primary layer of experience beneath the level at which we have explicitly posited spatial relations and objects with objective properties. The positional acts arise only against a background of nonpositional, autonomous experience:

> In the natural attitude, I do not have *perceptions*, I do not posit objects, one beside the other in their objective relations; instead, I have a stream of experiences which imply one another and account for one another—in their simultaneity as well as in their succession. . . . A first perception, based on no previous ground, is inconceivable. All perception presupposes a determinate past of the perceiving subject, and the abstract function of perception, as an encounter with *objects*, implies a more secret act by which we elaborate our milieu. (PP 281, 325)

* * *

Spatiality is related to our way of being implanted in the world. Accordingly, for different modalities of implantation, there will be different types of spatiality. For example, in the night, when the world of clear and articulate objects is cut off, we experience a peculiar spatiality without things. We can also speak of the spatiality of dreams, mythical spatiality, the spatiality of the schizophrenic, the spatiality of the work of art.

These various types of spatiality are not merely distortions of a single geometrical space. Each has its own originality. Nevertheless, they are not just private worlds, hermetically sealed. Instead, they communicate (for example, dreams and myth), because they all open onto that spatiality by which we are rooted in the natural world. They are variant ways of being inserted into one and the same world.

iv. Part Two of the *Phenomenology of Perception*: Chapter 3. The Thing and the Natural World

Merleau-Ponty's theory of perception is set over against the view that perception is not autonomous, not self-sufficient, but that, in order actually to take place, it must be accompanied by thought. This view becomes dominant at numerous junctures in the history of philosophy. It is especially transparent in Kant, for whom the senses present only a fragmented manifold that must be synthesized through a connection with thought. In particular, thought contributes the forms of unity (the categories) that must be imposed on the sensible manifold in order for experience or knowledge to be possible.

It is this conception of experience that Merleau-Ponty calls into question. In opposition to it, he wants to establish that "I perceive with my body" (PP 238, 275; 326, 376). That is to say, the bodily-perceptual dimension is a genuine autonomous locus for the emergence of meaning. In other words, perception proceeds autonomously at a level beneath and independent of the order of thought. An act of thought does not have to be invoked in order to account for perception.

We have encountered this issue already as a problem of synthesis, specifically as the problem of showing that the synthesis by which the subject is linked to the world is not a synthesis performed by thought or consciousness. In the chapter on "The Thing and the Natural World," Merleau-Ponty offers his definitive account of this synthesis. The account must, first of all, show that there is no necessity to invoke consciousness and thought in order to make perception possible. Let us see how Merleau-Ponty proceeds.

Suppose we are in the natural attitude. Here we "live" in the perceptual object. Suppose I am looking at a die. I do not see certain signs (profiles, properties) that allow me to make some inference to the die. I see the die itself.

Suppose now that I begin to think about my perception (reflect on it). That is, suppose I cease merely living in the object and try to take myself as a perceiving subject into account. I then immediately begin to have reservations about what I see, and I carry out a series of reductions:

(1) The die is only something for me. Perhaps other people nearby do not see it. It ceases to be in-itself and becomes merely a pole of my perceptual experience.

(2) I observe the die only through sight, so really all I am given is the outer surface. The die loses its density, its materiality, and becomes a mere visual spectacle. Thus all I really perceive are certain properties: size, shape, color.

(3) I do not see the die from all sides simultaneously. I do not really see its cubical shape but only certain distorted faces of the die.

(4) Finally, what is really received, really registered on my sense organs are only sensations, and these are no longer properties of the thing at all but merely modifications of my own body.

Now, having arrived at this point, how do I account for perception? I need to reconstruct the object, beginning with sensations: hence, the problem of synthesis.

The tradition would invoke a consciousness which is able to bring under its gaze this material given by the body, to survey it and link it together by a synthesis at the level of thought. This invocation is exactly what Merleau-Ponty rejects. He maintains that such a procedure "substitutes for the thing itself in its originary being an imperfect reconstitution of the thing out of subjective scraps" (PP 325, 375).

It is a substitution with momentous consequences:

First, the thing, since it is constructed by my thought, lies fully arrayed, spread out before me. Consequently, I cannot account for its opaqueness and transcendence.

Second, perception ceases to be inherent in an individual subject and the point of view of that subject. Rather, the consciousness performing the synthesis is able to range over all points of view and hence occupies no standpoint.

Then if we do not invoke such an act of thought, how are we to account for perception, for synthesis? We must show that the synthesis consciousness is otherwise called upon to perform is carried out within the bodily-perceptual dimension itself. In other words, the body is, in a sense, the agent of the synthesis. But everything depends on our grasping precisely in what sense! Merleau-Ponty does not simply transfer to the body the synthetic activity traditionally assigned to consciousness; he does not simply substitute the body for consciousness. That would be impossible because the body is not aloof from things as is consciousness; instead, the body is "saturated with its objects."

Because of this saturation, because the body is not an agent of synthesis which stands aloof from what it synthesizes, we cannot distinguish between a material synthesized (mere content) and the activity of synthesizing. We saw this in the discussion of sensation. It is not as though discrete sensations are first given and then structured. Instead, the very reception already involves a response, and the structuration is always already under way. Pure, discrete sensation is an abstraction.

So, in general, the synthesis is always already under way; it is a "synthesis in dialogue." To distinguish discrete elements devoid of synthetic connection is to deal in abstractions. There are no such discrete elements and thus no need for a synthetic activity to be applied to them externally (whether that activity is one of the body or of consciousness).

Recall the analysis that reduced perception to sensation:

(1) object-for-me (object ceases to be in-itself, loses its transcendence)
(2) properties
(3) profiles
(4) sensations.

Merleau-Ponty wants to show that this reduction is an *abstraction* and that therefore no *separate* synthetic activity has to be invoked to fill gaps. In positive terms: he begins with profiles and retraces the constitution of the object, showing how at each level a synthesis is already in play and how each level leads to the next without an explicit act of synthesis.

a.) From profiles to properties.

Consider the size and shape of something perceived. They vary with our perspective. But we do not attribute these variations to the thing itself. Instead, we think the thing has its true shape and size. On what do we base this belief?

One explanation would be that as a matter of convention we regard as true the size the object has when within reach. Likewise, the true shape is the one the object presents when in a plane parallel to our frontal elevation. These provide the standards for dismissing the others as mere appearance.

What is presupposed here is that we somehow have all variant shapes and sizes "spread out" before us, so that it is simply a matter of choosing one as the standard. But that is not faithful to our experience; it already places our experience in an objective context.

The thing seen at a distance is the same thing (with the same size), now seen farther away; it is not seen as smaller. The plate seen obliquely is perceived not as an ellipse but as a circular plate viewed obliquely. Thus in perception there is already a constant size and shape throughout perspectival variation, which suggests another explanation of perceptual constancy: in perception I already take into account my own perspective. How could I do so?

Perhaps perception involves a system of laws which correlate the given profile and the conditions under which it is presented, so that what is seen remains constant. But this would amount to saying that what is given is subsumed under a law. Thereby the object of perception becomes something thought rather than perceived.

Merleau-Ponty wants to account for perceptual constancy without resorting to a thought that would maintain it. He notes that for every object, there is an optimal distance and direction for viewing it. In other words, there is a privileged appearance (privileged size and shape) which I obtain from a certain preferred perspective. But this privileged appearance is not simply chosen. Instead, it is that appearance in which the thing most fully yields itself up to my viewing (with a balance between the inner and outer horizon and a maximum of clarity and articulation). The point is that this privileged appearance is specified by the object, not by some choice on the part of the perceiver.

All other appearances are drawn into the privileged one (cf. the example of the plate), thereby ensuring the unity of the experience of size and shape. It is not a matter of the application of a law. On the contrary, when the object is viewed obliquely I feel a tension, a lack of balance in the world on which I already have an established grip through my body.

Thus we give an abstract account of perception when we explain it as a synthesis of discrete profiles. There are no discrete, separate profiles posited in experience. We are never *simply* confined to a single profile; every profile stands out against an inner horizon of other profiles. So a single profile is not a discrete element which I would have to connect with subsequently seen profiles: "I do not have one perspectival view and then another, the two joined together by the intellect; on the contrary, each perspective *passes into* the other, and, if we can still speak of synthesis here, it is a 'synthesis of transition'" (PP 329, 380).

Profiles are connected from the very beginning, and each profile opens onto a totality of profiles, onto the thing seen from everywhere. Furthermore, the profiles are already polarized toward a revelation of the object, of its true size and shape: "I am not conscious of my perceptual deportments, each for itself; they are given to me only implicitly, as stages of the gesture leading to the optimal deportment. Likewise, the corresponding perspectival views are not posited before me discretely, one after the other, but offer themselves only as points of passage leading to the thing itself in its own size and shape" (PP 303, 349).

b.) From properties to the object.

We have reached the level at which there are properties, not merely profiles. At this point, the hitherto dominant view would invoke a synthetic activity of consciousness to bind the properties together in relation to the object itself. The object would be taken as a *meant unity*, a signification not given in perception, a signification accessible only to thought.

Merleau-Ponty wants to avoid this invocation of thought and wants to show, as he says regarding color, that "perception bypasses the colors and proceeds directly to the thing; thus we perceive the expression on a face without noting the color of the eyes" (PP 305, 352). In other words, just as our perception passes through profiles to the true size and shape, so it passes through properties to the thing. Properties are already, in perception itself, linked together and linked to the object. So it is not necessary to call in a synthesizing activity.

That is apparent as soon as we attend to the phenomena and abandon the abstract view that would build up the world out of different configurations of a standard set of color-qualities or, in other words, as soon as we abandon the view of color as a mere quality exemplified in many individuals. Merleau-Ponty offers this example: the wooly red of the carpet would literally not be the same red if it were not the red of this particular thing. Color is linked to the thing.

Merleau-Ponty elaborates this linkage among properties and with the object. He cites an experiment in which one looks at a feebly lighted white wall. To unhampered vision, the wall appears white. But if one looks at it through a small opening in a screen which hides the source of light, then the wall appears bluish-gray.

What happens here is that the small patch of wall seen through the opening is torn out of its context and becomes just a patch of color, not the color of a wall. Also, it loses its relation to the lighting. Merleau-Ponty concludes: the color seen, the articulation of the field (including sizes and shapes), and the lighting are connected.

Of special importance is the phenomenon of lighting (the illumination of the spectacle, the configuration of shadows and reflections). Lighting is not seen but allows us to see the rest of the spectacle. The lighting remains in the background but in such a way as to lead our gaze. It directs our gaze, anticipates our vision. Vision takes up what is traced out by the lighting. That is, the lighting guides the articulation of the field and the revelation of spatial properties (size, shape).

But this articulation of the field (following the lighting) is not a matter of interpreting or synthesizing sensible "givens." The lighting is not given, not actually seen. Instead, what is involved here is the body which is already immersed in the world and in the structures of the world, which already knows its way around, and which is capable of responding to the promptings of the light.

Merleau-Ponty also points to the well-known fact that the general illumination in a given context is always taken as the norm. In a room illuminated by electric light (yellow), this light comes to function as neutral (comparable to daylight), and the whole color spectrum then shifts. In other words, the colors of things are determined in relation to what is taken as neutral light. Again, what is involved is not interpretation but bodily engagement.

Thus there are connections among the various features or properties of the perceived spectacle. There is a logic of the spectacle. I do not grasp independent properties which would need to be connected. Rather, in their very nature they are already connected. What a property (such as color) is is not independent of its relation to other properties. All the properties form a total interconnected system:

> The colors of the visual field form a system, one ordered around a dominant: namely, the lighting taken as a level. We now glimpse a deeper sense pertaining to the organization of the field: not only the colors, but also the geometric characteristics, all the sensory givens, and the meaning of objects form a system. Our perception in its entirety is animated by a logic that assigns to each object all its determinations in function of the determinations of the other objects and that "deletes," as unreal, every aberrant given. Our perception is entirely subtended by the certitude of the world. (PP 313, 361)

Merleau-Ponty says in the same vein that "a thing would not have this color if it did not also have this form, these tactile properties, this sonority, and this odor" (PP 319, 368).

Now we need to go one step further: What about the object itself? The object used to be taken as a meant unity, a signification (accessible only to thought) which served as a substratum for the unification of properties. But now we recognize properties as already connected from their very inception. Color is already linked to the total field. So there is no need to call in an act of thought that would posit a signification in reference to which the properties could be connected. What then about the object itself, the significative unity? Merleau-Ponty wants to say that it is already there in perception. Color (for example) is not some free-floating quality that would have to be connected to the object: "color in living perception is an introduction into the thing" (PP 305, 352).

So how is the object itself to be understood? It is no longer a thought-unity beyond the properties but a certain *style* immanent in them:

> The unity of the thing, beyond all its fixed properties, is not a substrate, an empty X, a sheer bearer of the inherence, but is that unique accent found in each of the properties, that unique manner of existing of which the properties are a secondary expression. For example, the fragility, rigidity, transparency, and crystalline sound of glass translate one single mode of being. . . . The thing is penetrated by a symbolism that binds every sensory quality to the others. (PP 319, 368)

> We comprehend a thing the same way we comprehend some novel behavior: not by way of the intellectual operation of subsumption but by appropriating the mode of existence delineated in the observable signs there before us. (PP 319, 369)

> The meaning of a thing inhabits that thing the way the soul inhabits the body: the meaning is not behind the appearances, and the meaning of the ashtray (at least its total and individual meaning, as given in perception) is not a certain

idea of the ashtray which would coordinate all its sensory aspects and would be accessible only to the understanding. The meaning of the ashtray animates the ashtray through and through, incarnates itself in the ashtray with the clearest evidence. That is why we say perception offers us the thing "in person" or "in flesh and blood." (PP 319–20, 369)

c.) From the object-for-me to the object-in-itself.

Thus far we have described the object only as correlative to the body and to the perceptual life of the body. But that is not sufficient. For, first, we cannot simply ground the unity of the object in the unity of the body. The reason is that the body is not simply a given unity. The body ceases to be an obscure mass and becomes a genuine unity only when it moves toward things, only when it is intentionally projected outward. Second, the object does not simply present itself as for my perception. Instead, it presents itself as in-itself: "the thing is oblivious of us and rests in itself" (PP 322, 372).

So how are we to account for the transcendence of the object? How can there be an in-itself-for-us? A clue is found in the notion of meaning that Merleau-Ponty has developed. The object, the significative unity, is not grasped in its entirety, as would be a meaning posited by thought. Rather, the disclosure of the object, instead of operating beyond the sensible aspects, beyond appearances, takes place in and through them.

But the sensible aspects, inasmuch as they are connected with a standpoint, are never fully revealed. Meaning is never fully revealed; the object is inexhaustible: "The very meaning of the thing crystallizes under our eyes, and this is a meaning no verbal analysis can exhaust, a meaning identical with the very exhibition of the evidence of the thing" (PP 323, 373).

A total appearance is never achieved, and the meaning of a thing is thus never fully revealed. This meaning is not something fully revealed to thought; instead, it "gets built up before our eyes."

We could say that the thing holds itself in reserve; this is its peculiar transcendence, its holding itself aloof from us, remaining oblivious of us. But we need to go one step further.

Appearances (the disclosure of the meaning of the thing) do not simply unfold before me as though I were a disinterested spectator. I have to "reach out" for the thing in a movement of my body or with my gaze (for instance, when my vision takes up the articulation of the field which is *already* traced out by the lighting), and thereby the transcendent character of the thing is accentuated.

Now, how is my gaze able to take up the object and disclose it? The reason is that the object always stands out against a world and, moreover, my body is always already acquainted with the "logic" of that world: "A thing is not forcefully *given* in perception; it is internally appropriated by us, reconstituted and lived by us, insofar as it is attached to (and is merely one of the possible concretions of) a world whose fundamental structures we bear in ourselves. Even as lived by us, the thing is no less transcendent to our life, for the human body, with its dispositions, ones that sketch round about it a human environment, is traversed by a movement toward the world itself" (PP 326–27, 377).

* * *

So if we interrogate perception, what we find is not unorganized material or profiles or properties, all needing to be synthesized. On the contrary, we find objects disclosing themselves. And beneath this, as its support, we find, not consciousness, but rather being-in-the-world, the primordial bodily anchorage in the world.

Finally, what is this world toward which the body has an inherent movement and in which it is anchored? It is not just a collection of all objects, things in the objective sense, objects appearing to a disinterested spectator. No one could be engaged in such a world.

The world is not some cognitive meaning, an idea. Instead it is presupposed by all cognitive activity. Merleau-Ponty says it is "not possible to conceive of a subject without a world" (PP 328, 379).

Yet that is just the difficulty when we want to say what the world is. Not only are we always already bound up within the world, but it is the already presupposed basis for all description, all saying.

According to Husserl, the world is the always already presupposed foundation of all affirmations and denials—not only judgmental but also perceptual ones. Whatever we doubt or describe is set against the background of an enduring belief in the world. That is, the *Urdoxa,* the *Urglaube,* the horizon of all horizons.

* * *

To conclude, Merleau-Ponty's whole effort here has been to refute the results of the reflection we carried out initially, whereby we reduced the thing to sensations. He has tried to show that such reflection is abstract and inappropriate.

Yet, if Merleau-Ponty in effect vindicates the natural attitude as it was prior to reflection, he does not do so by simply remaining in that attitude. On the contrary, he can demonstrate the inadequacy of the reflection only through another reflection, one which, rather than dissolving the perceptual dimension into a passively received material and a form-giving activity, brings to light the holistic character of that dimension. This other reflection is to accord with the fundamental ambiguity of the perceptual dimension. What is this new type of reflection?

v. Interlude: Review and Preview

Let us return to the statement from *The Visible and the Invisible* we quoted at the outset: "The end of a philosophy is the account of its beginning."

We have taken up the beginning of Merleau-Ponty's thought and have observed that this beginning takes place as a phenomenology of perception, a description of the pre-objective domain of perceptual experience. Yet, Merleau-Ponty says at end of this descriptive inquiry: "To phenomenology understood as direct description, there must be added a phenomenology of phenomenology" (PP 365, 419). This phenomenology of phenomenology, whose goal is to define a new kind of comprehension and reflection, is precisely that which could give an account of the beginning and to that extent would constitute the end of Merleau-Ponty's philosophy.

That task is undertaken in the last part of the *Phenomenology of Perception* and then is extended in Merleau-Ponty's later writings. What will be most important is to grasp the essential questions Merleau-Ponty comes to take up.

Let us review the character of Merleau-Ponty's project, review the way he works out that project up to the point we have reached in our study, and preview the further developments of the problematic.

(1) The project.

The *Phenomenology of Perception* is an attempt to reverse, to undo, the objectification accomplished by modern science and philosophy. This objectification is one into which we are lured by perception itself. It is an objectification by which we lose ourselves in the things of experience in such a way as to lose sight of experience itself, namely, that by which there first come to be things for us.

In Husserlian terms, the task is to exercise an *epoché* with respect to the world of science and common sense so as to reveal beneath it the life-world. More specifically, the *Phenomenology of Perception* is an attempt to bring to light the pre-objective dimension of lived perceptual experience, that dimension in which we first have access to things, that dimension which is presupposed by objective thought and of which such thought is only a second-order expression.

Merleau-Ponty's goal, however, is not simply to bring this dimension to light. He also wants to establish something about it—its primacy. He wants to establish the primacy of perceptual experience. We have seen that three issues are involved in the thesis of the primacy of perception:

First, perceptual experience is *original*.

That means perception is not reducible to thought and the perceptual object is not reducible to the object of thought, to something constituted by thought. Instead, perception is such that it cannot simply be reenacted in reflective thought. In perceptual experience, there is an opaqueness that resists being grasped by reflection.

We have noted the enigma: reflection must show that something cannot be grasped by reflection.

Second, perceptual experience is *autonomous* with respect to thought.

That means perception is not only irreducible to thought but also does not presuppose thought. Perception is not in any way based on thought as its precondition.

Third, perceptual experience *founds* thought.

That means thought has its roots in perception, originates out of perception, and always retains its dependence on perception. Thus, in general terms, mind is radically dependent; reason has its roots in the pre-rational.

In this third issue the enigmatic character of the whole enterprise is most obtrusive. Consider: it is to be shown that thought is dependent. But if thought is dependent (is not pure), its results are compromised by that dependence. Since thought is tied to a standpoint, thought is relative. But then the very activity of thought, by which Merleau-Ponty will establish that thought is dependent, is itself dependent. Hence, its result ("thought is dependent") is compromised.

So the whole project recoils upon itself. If we establish by thought the dependence of thought, then it is required that the very establishing be called into question: the result renders questionable that very activity in which it is established.

Therefore, the project in the end has to return to its beginning; accordingly: "The end of a philosophy is the account of its beginning."

(2) Developments thus far.

Let us recall how Merleau-Ponty has brought to light the domain of perceptual experience.

First, his greatest effort has been to withdraw the body from the objective world of science. In *The Structure of Behavior* and Part One of the *Phenomenology of Perception*, Merleau-Ponty showed that the body cannot be conceived as a mere thing, as a mere seat of various causal processes. He has, thus, retrieved the phenomenal body, the body as lived, the subjectivized body. This retrieval of the phenomenal body has two major consequences.

By subjectivizing the body, Merleau-Ponty, in turn, renders consciousness radically incarnate. In particular, the perceptual subject is no longer to be regarded as a transcendental subject aloof from the world, a subject that constitutes the world by merely imposing form on formless, meaningless sense-material received passively by the body. Instead, the perceptual subject—as bodily—is a subject inherent in the world, saturated with its object. The perceptual subject represents an anonymous, pre-personal level beneath that of personal, volitional life.

Next, by withdrawing the body from the objective world, Merleau-Ponty withdraws from that world the things to which the body is intentionally connected. That is to say, Merleau-Ponty uncovers beneath objects in the scientific sense the genuine perceptual things with their gaps, ambiguity, indeterminacy, and dependence on context.

Against this background, Merleau-Ponty's problem was then to exhibit the character of the perceptual dimension in general: how it is that the perceptual subject and perceived things form a whole or a system. Otherwise put, the problem became one of synthesis, the problem of exhibiting that synthesis by which the subject and things are joined into a whole and by which the subject is present to actual things (rather than to mere sensations, profiles, or properties).

Near the end of our previous discussions, we considered in detail the character of this synthesis. Let us recall only its most important feature: it is not a synthesis performed by consciousness. Instead, it is a bodily synthesis, one of which the body is the agent. Yet this is not so in the sense that Merleau-Ponty simply ascribes to the body the synthetic activity traditionally assigned to consciousness. The body is not an agent of synthesis which stands aloof from what it synthesizes, merely imposing form on a pregiven material. On the contrary, the body is saturated with its objects, and no distinction can be drawn between a form (imposed by the body) and a material (merely given). The body responds to the way it is addressed by things. What we have here is a synthesis in dialogue.

Merleau-Ponty has thus brought to light the perceptual dimension, at least with respect to the relation of the subject to things, to the natural world. It is clear that by showing the bodily character of the perceptual synthesis, Merleau-Ponty has established the primacy of perceptual experience in the first two senses: originality and autonomy. He has succeeded in giving an account of perception without having to invoke an act of thought as a precondition.

(3) Preview of further developments.

At this point Merleau-Ponty has obviously established only part of what was projected. Let us try to gain a preview of the necessary further development of the problematic.

Merleau-Ponty has accounted for the inherence of the subject in the natural world. But I exist not only in a natural world but also in a social world, a world in which many things are not mere natural objects but are cultural objects, things overlaid with specifically human or cultural meaning. And, most importantly, I exist in the world with others. I perceive not only things but also other people.

Thus it is incumbent on Merleau-Ponty to take up the problem of the experience of other people, the problem of intersubjectivity (last chapter of Part Two).

Yet it is still not sufficient to deal only with the relation of the subject to things and to other subjects. For the subject is also related to itself, is to some degree capable of self-consciousness. Consciousness is for-itself, and that is what most of all distinguishes it from things.

The act in which the subject is conscious of itself is what in modern philosophy is called the *cogito*. It is then under this title that Merleau-Ponty takes up the problem of self-consciousness in the first chapter of Part Three. Furthermore, it is in this context that he seeks to establish the third sense of the primacy of perception: that thought is founded on perceptual experience.

The two subsequent chapters then bring the *Phenomenology of Perception* to an appropriate conclusion. In a sense, the chapter on temporality draws together Merleau-Ponty's entire conception of (finite) subjectivity, as we would expect in light of his cryptic statement that subjectivity *is* temporality. In the final chapter ("Freedom") Merleau-Ponty brings philosophy—abruptly—into relation with the nonphilosophical: he poses the question of the transition to praxis.

From the point of view of his later works, the chapter on the *cogito* is the end of the *Phenomenology of Perception*—in the sense that it, most of all, poses the question of giving an account of beginnings, of executing a return to beginnings. This is evident if we observe that the subject's relation to itself is nothing other than reflection.

The entire *Phenomenology of Perception* has proceeded, by reflection, up to that point where reflection itself finally becomes an explicit problem, which is to say that in the chapter on the *cogito* the *Phenomenology of Perception* becomes a problem for itself. In other words, here we are confronted with the project of a phenomenology *of* phenomenology.

What then are we to say of the later works, especially *The Visible and the Invisible*? I suggest that they do not abandon the project initiated in the *Phenomenology of Perception*. On the contrary, they take it up in a more radical way.

Initially, an elaborate restatement of the project is given in the first two essays collected in English in *The Primacy of Perception and Other Essays on Phenomenological Psychology, the Philosophy of Art, History and Politics*.

Next, the inquiry into language is renewed in *Signs*. We have seen already to what degree the problem of the primacy of perception (specifically, the founded character of thought) centers on the problem of language.

Finally, we find in Merleau-Ponty a renewed discussion of the problem of thought and reflection and, coordinated with this, a deepening of the inquiry into the *logos* of the sensible world. These developments are evident in "The Philosopher and His Shadow," "Eye and Mind," and *The Visible and the Invisible*.[1]

In what sense do the later works take up the earlier project more radically? In what way do they deepen the whole inquiry?

In "The Philosopher and His Shadow," Merleau-Ponty speaks of his project not in terms of the primacy of perception but in terms of "an ontological

---

1 *The Visible and the Invisible* is treated comprehensively in John Sallis, *Phenomenology and the Return to Beginnings* (Pittsburgh, PA: Duquesne University Press, 1973), reissued with a new introduction by the author (2003).

rehabilitation of the sensible" (S 167, 210). In the first working note printed in *The Visible and the Invisible*, he writes of the "necessity of a return to ontology" (VI 165, 219). And in another note he describes philosophy itself as "Being speaking within us" (VI 197, 250).

On the basis of such clues, let me suggest that the deepening is most of all an attempt to bring the project of the *Phenomenology of Perception* into the dimension of *fundamental ontology*.

vi. Part Two of the *Phenomenology of Perception*: Chapter 4. Other People and the Human World

Today I want to address to you some words about experiencing other people.

This is a curious problem, a curious problem to speak to others about. For, in speaking about it—certainly in speaking about it to others—I already take for granted the possibility of genuine communication with other people. It is as Merleau-Ponty says: "I can formulate a solipsistic philosophy, but, in so doing, I presuppose a linguistic community of humans, and I address myself to this community" (PP 360, 414).

So in a sense I already prejudge the issue, already assume *that* there is an actual experience of others, whereby the problem is only: *how* is it possible? And if you objected to my prejudging the issue in this way, you could never convince me. For you could convince me (genuinely communicate to me) only at the cost of denying in action what you are saying in words.

Therefore, I prejudge the issue. Yet this prejudgment is no *mere* assumption. At the very least, it is an assumption to which our inquiry should allow us to return. That is, the inquiry itself ought to make possible a return to its own questionable beginnings.

* * *

Let me evoke a scene to initiate our inquiry.

I am looking out from a second-story window. As my gaze moves from what is near out toward the horizon, I see a variety of things. First, I perceive the top of a tree that is in my yard. Beyond the tree are the roofs and upper portions of houses, hidden partially behind one another, with short stretches of what I know to be streets. Beyond that is a field I saw being cultivated several months ago, and in the middle of it stands a farmhouse with its various outbuildings. Beyond that are clumps of trees which, as I look toward the horizon, coalesce into brownish-gray patches I know to be woods.

It is not a pleasant day. It is cold, damp, and drizzly. I see no people, no activity, and no immediate evidence that the houses are human habitations. But the houses *are* different, different from the tree in my yard and the woods in the distance. And the difference is not a matter of shape, color, or any of the usual perceptual qualities.

Just then a child appears, dashes across a street, and disappears behind a house that blocks my view. There is a suddenness—almost something uncanny—about his appearance on this scene. His appearance crystallizes the difference between the houses and the distant woods, the difference I previously only felt.

Yet the difference is still difficult to articulate: houses are places where people live. It is not that people could not live in the woods, but the houses are nothing other than places for human habitation. They are made for that purpose.

Here my articulation already tempts me to abandon what I see. In seeing the houses, I do not reflect on the intentions of those who built them. I do not even *see*, in the strict sense, that people do live in them. At the moment, I see no people. Yet I feel somehow the houses are different. They radiate a kind of meaning I do not feel in the case of the distant woods, and, try as I may, I cannot see houses as mere natural things. I can say of the houses what Merleau-Ponty says: "Each one exudes an atmosphere of humanity" (PP 347, 400). That is why the sudden appearance of the child served to crystallize what I felt in my perception of the houses.

The houses are not just natural things. They are cultural objects; they radiate an atmosphere of humanity, without my having to evoke this atmosphere explicitly. They present themselves immediately as relics betraying the existence of other people. Merleau-Ponty says: "In a cultural object, I feel the imminent presence of others under a veil of anonymity" (PP 348, 400).

For us city dwellers it is especially difficult to notice what is distinctive about our experience of cultural objects, to notice how such things offer us the presence of other people and betray the entire social dimension. It is difficult because we live so much in the midst of cultural objects. In most rooms we can scarcely see a single thing that is not a cultural object. We are so immersed in the social world that we lack the contrast between it and the natural world. Or, to put it better, our natural world is the social world.

Perhaps this confusion of human things with natural things has something to do with the dehumanization of the technology-dominated city. For us the countryside (natural world) can seem more human than the social world of the city.

* * *

"In a cultural object, I feel the imminent presence of others under a veil of anonymity." Objective thought does not take this feeling very seriously and maintains that original perception is perception of mere things. If there is some further content involved in the experience of cultural objects, it must be something simply added by association. That is, if I see a house as having a social meaning—as not a mere thing—it is only because in the past I have observed that houses are generally used by people for certain purposes.

But this is clearly no solution, because what I have *seen* in the past are not other people making use of houses! Strictly speaking, can we say that there is any sense in which I *see other people*? How could I experience another consciousness? Consciousness is not a perceptual object. Consciousness can be known only from the inside—the way I know myself. But I cannot know the other from the inside without becoming that other, and then he would no longer be other but just myself.

So I do not experience the consciousness of another. All I perceive are bodies which I take to be the bodies of other people. But why I do take them thus? Would I not be equally justified in taking them as mere robots? That is what Descartes wondered.

Therefore, the problem of cultural objects—of accounting for that atmosphere of humanity which surrounds them—leads back to the problem of the body of the other person, that is, to the problem of "the very first of the cultural objects, the one in virtue of which all the rest exist" (PP 348, 401). How is it that a body is experienced as the body *of* another person?

We are told that this experience is the result of an inference by analogy. I compare the gestures of others with my own and by analogy *infer* that there is another consciousness behind those gestures, just as there is behind my own. But what would ever lead me—much less an infant—to make this comparison unless I *already* experienced a body *as* the body of another? How much similarity is there between the gestures of another, gestures I see from the outside, and my own gestures as I experience them from within?

Furthermore, the experience of another is not the product of any such sophisticated reasoning. I do not infer to the existence of the other; I recognize the other immediately. A smile is not a sign I use in order to infer, behind it, another person. Rather, I perceive the other person *in* the smile. In that smile the other person is present to me.

But how is this possible? How can the other person be present to me in my perception of his body?

* * *

In a "Working Note" for *The Visible and the Invisible*, Merleau-Ponty says: "What is interesting is not an expedient to solve the 'problem of the other'—It is a transformation of the problem" (VI 269, 322). This raises two questions: Why does the problem need to be transformed? And what kind of transformation does Merleau-Ponty propose?

A transformation is necessary because the problem—in the only way it can be formulated within the framework of traditional philosophy—is insoluble. Any proposed solution is actually only an expedient, not a solution. Let us see why.

For transcendental philosophy, consciousness is simply for-itself and constitutes its own objects. But if I constitute the world, then there cannot be in that world a genuine other, an other not constituted by me: "If I constitute the world, I cannot think another consciousness, for that consciousness, too, would have to have constituted the world, and, at least with respect to this other point of view on the world, I would not be the constituting consciousness. Even if I succeeded in thinking the other consciousness as one that constitutes the world, it would still be I who constituted that consciousness as having such a power, and so I would again be the only constituting consciousness" (PP 350, 402).

So how does Merleau-Ponty propose to transform the problem? He does so by recasting it within the framework of the conception of finite subjectivity (being-in-the-world) that the *Phenomenology of Perception* has elaborated.

We need to recall a basic feature of this conception. Let us begin with the fundamental dualism of modern philosophy: mind versus body. In early modern philosophy, this dualism is absolute; consciousness and body are absolutely distinct, and there is no merging of one into the other. The result is that subjectivity is identified as pure consciousness, and the body is identified as a mere thing. The body is then regarded either as existing self-sufficiently (as substance) alongside consciousness (in such a way that their relation is unintelligible) or as simply constituted by consciousness. (There is also the alternative of empiricism which simply inverts the entire schema and identifies the subject with the body-thing and disposes of consciousness in whatever way it can.)

Merleau-Ponty opposes this entire tradition, primarily on the ground that it fails to do justice to the body. As a result, it ascribes to consciousness an autonomy, a purity, which is excessive. It thus fails to account for the dependence of mind, the radical finitude of subjectivity.

So it is through a reinterpretation of the body that Merleau-Ponty initiates his conception of subjectivity. And it is thus that he overthrows the old dualism. How does Merleau-Ponty proceed? He shows that the objective conception of the body is an abstraction, a second-order construction obtained by impoverishing the genuine phenomenon, namely, the body as lived, the body as one's own.

The result is that Merleau-Ponty withdraws the body from the objective world and places it on the side of the subject, on the side of perceptual consciousness. Perceptual consciousness becomes a bodily consciousness, not a pure consciousness standing behind the body to which the body would, at most, merely transmit sensations. Furthermore, perceptual consciousness *as bodily* is a consciousness which is in-the-world, which is always already committed to the world, and which always already knows its way around prior to all explicit acts and decisions and prior to all explicit knowledge.

Thus Merleau-Ponty reintroduces a new dualism *within subjectivity*: The first pole is perceptual, bodily existence which is caught up in the world and by virtue of which a world is always already present to us prior to any explicit acts. This level has a kind of anonymity. It runs its course beneath the level of personal existence, explicit decision, thought, self-consciousness. So I say not that *I* perceive but that *one* perceives.

But not all modes of consciousness are of this character. There is also the pole of personal existence, explicit decision, thought, self-consciousness. Thus Merleau-Ponty replaces the traditional dualism of substances (body and conscious subject) with a new dualism of levels within subjectivity. But this new dualism is not absolute. The distinction is relativized: the body and consciousness are not two substances but two moments or poles within the structure of existence. The relation between them is a founding relation: the bodily-perceptual moment founds the personal one. It sustains it by providing an articulated world, by laying down a world, within which our personal acts are executed. Our personal acts do go beyond the bodily but remain tied to it.

* * *

It is in terms of this conception of subjectivity that Merleau-Ponty wants to recast the problem of the other. Thus he proceeds in three stages:

(1) He treats the problem of the other in relation to the bodily-perceptual pole. This yields a solution to the problem of the other.
(2) The other pole—that of personal consciousness, self-consciousness—is introduced, and this destroys the "solution" provided by the first stage.
(3) Finally, the two poles are brought together, the relation between them is reinstated, and the results of the first two stages are brought to synthesis.

In different terms, the stages are:

(1) The other for pre-personal existence
(2) The other for personal existence
(3) The other for the subject as a whole

(1) The other for pre-personal existence.

Merleau-Ponty has uncovered a pre-personal level of existence by withdrawing the body from the objective world and placing it on the side of the subject. The result is that perceptual consciousness loses its purity and transparency and becomes an incarnate consciousness. It is no longer a consciousness aloof from the body, imposing form on material transmitted by the body. Instead, perceptual consciousness genuinely inheres in the body and through the body is engaged in the world. That is, the perceptual subject is nothing other than a movement toward the world, a pattern of behavior, a certain hold on the world.

If this is so, then in the perceived body of an other I find not just some external sign from which to infer the existence of another person, but rather a genuine *trace* of another consciousness. The other perceptual subject is not behind but present in that behavior, those gestures, which I see. According to Merleau-Ponty: "I know unquestionably that that man over there *sees*, that my sensible world is also his, because *I am present at his seeing*, his seeing *is visible* in his eyes' grasp of the scene" (S 169, 214).

Because this level is pre-personal, there are no real obstacles between subjects. I meet the other in the world, and we communicate through the common world in which we are both engaged. Indeed, my perspective on the world is not the same as the other's, but just as in individual perception my various perspectives on an object blend and coalesce into the object itself, so my perspective and that of the other blend into the unity of a common world:

> We have learned with respect to individual perception that our perspectival views cannot be posited apart from one another; we know that they flow into one another and are unified in the thing. It is in these terms, that is to say, in terms of one and the same world, that we must likewise conceive of the communication between consciousnesses. In reality, the other is not enclosed within my perspective on the world, because this perspective itself has no definite limits, because it spontaneously flows into the other's perspective, and because these perspectives are unified in a single world, the one in which we both participate as anonymous perceiving subjects.... My perspective flows into his, his into mine, and we coexist through one single world. (PP 353–54, 405–7)

We experience this most vividly in dialogue. There our words are interwoven so as to reveal what we are discussing and indeed reveal it in a way neither of us would be capable of alone. The dialogue is the product of neither of us individually. Likewise, in perception our perspectives on the world coalesce; I and the other are simply different moments of a single pre-personal, anonymous existence:

> My body is precisely what perceives the other's body, and it finds there something like a miraculous prolongation of its own intentions; it finds a familiar way of dealing with the world. Just as the parts of my body together form a system, so too the other's body and mine are henceforth a unitary whole, merely the back and the front of one and the same phenomenon. Likewise, the anonymous existence of which my body is at every moment the trace henceforth inhabits these two bodies at once. (PP 354, 406).

(2) The other for personal existence.

The problem would seem to be solved. Yet Merleau-Ponty now abruptly asks: "Is it at all, however, properly speaking, an *other* that we now attain?" (PP 355, 408). Merleau-Ponty then continues: "What we have done, in sum, is this: we have leveled down the I and the Thou to one experience with two poles, we have introduced the impersonal into the center of subjectivity, we have abolished the individuality of perspectives. In this general confusion, however, have we not eliminated the ego and, with it, the alter ego?" (PP 355, 408).

According to the account given at the first stage, I perceive the other as a portion of behavior. But the behavior as I see it is still not that other person. For instance, I perceive his anger in his behavior, but that anger does not have the same significance for me as it has for him; the anger is displayed for me, lived for him.

Consider also the question of communication. If both of us are merely anonymous (with no distinction of persons), then when we communicate and discover a common world, a question still arises: *Who* communicates and for *whom* does this world exist? The point is that the subject is not simply—in fact, never totally—a pre-personal, anonymous openness onto the world. Instead, consciousness is always also personal. This entails two circumstances:

First, consciousness is also presence to itself (self-consciousness). But, if so, then how do I ever experience the other? Certainly I do not perceive the other's presence to himself.

Second, objects are always objects-for-consciousness, even though they are not simply products of my constitutive activity, even though they are always already there: "My own acts always surpass me, and I wallow in generality; nevertheless, I myself am the one by whom these acts are lived" (PP 358, 411).

So again the problem arises: How can there be a genuine other who is still for me? As soon as we introduce the personal dimension into consciousness, we are led back again to solipsism: "There is a lived solipsism here, and it simply cannot be surmounted" (PP 358, 411).

(3) The other for the subject as a whole.

The two reflections have yielded contradictory results. We have discovered the presence of the other in pre-personal life only to find that presence destroyed at the personal level. We cannot accept either conclusion as final.

Indeed, there is a solipsism in experience inasmuch as I never experience the other's presence to himself. Yet Merleau-Ponty adds: "Nevertheless, the other is immediately, if not fully, meaningful to me" (PP 359, 412).

The other must be to some degree absent. Yet he can be absent only if he is also in some sense present, revealed to me:

Solitude and communication cannot be two horns of a dilemma but must be two moments of a single phenomenon, since the other does in fact exist for me. . . . My experience must in some way give me the other, since, if it did not, I could not even speak of solitude and could not at all declare the other inaccessible. What is initially given and true is . . . the straining of my experience toward an other, one whose existence on the horizon of my life is incontestable, even if my knowledge of his existence is imperfect. (PP 359, 412–13)

But how is this possible? How in spite of the other's absence can he still in some way be present?

We have considered the other from the points of view of the pre-personal and the personal. But there we were proceeding abstractly, for in fact the pre-personal and personal are always intertwined. We know already how to bring them together: the personal always has its roots in the pre-personal. It is always already inscribed in the world, already situated, through the agency of the pre-personal.

Let us then see how, correspondingly, Merleau-Ponty brings together the seemingly contradictory results of his two reflections. He says: "I find myself already situated and engaged in a physical and social world" (PP 360, 413). That means the other, the social, is always already there. Differently put, my personal existence always stands out from a pre-personal background which already inserts me into the social world and through which the other is already discovered. I am always already open to the social. According to Merleau-Ponty: "The social is already there for us prior to our taking it up in knowledge or judgment. . . . Before we take it up into full consciousness, the social exists for us as an inarticulate solicitation" (PP 362, 415). Furthermore: "Our relation to the social, like our relation to the world in general, is deeper than all explicit perception and all judgment. . . . We must return to the social just as we are in contact with it by the sheer fact that we exist and just as we are bound to it prior to all objectification" (PP 362, 415).

Yet we must observe that this does not remove all barriers to communication. However much the other may be already there, I still have no experience of his presence to himself: "Just as the instant of my death is for me an inaccessible future, so it is afortiori certain that I never live the presence of the other to himself. Nonetheless, every other exists for me in the guise of an incontrovertible style or milieu of coexistence, and my life has a social atmosphere just as it savors of mortality" (PP 364, 418).

That presence of the other which lies at the root of all communication is what is involved in our pre-personal engagement in the common world. Thus Merleau-Ponty points out that to the extent each of us withdraws from engagement in the world into the core of our thinking nature, we approximate the condition of solipsism and communication breaks down. That is to say, when the other just stares at me, he reduces me to a mere object in his world. But just let him speak or undertake some action together with me, and he ceases to be totally transcendent and inaccessible: "Solipsism would be true in the strict sense only of someone who succeeded in tacitly observing his own existence without being anything and without doing anything, which is of course impossible, since existence is being-in-the-world" (PP 361, 414–15).

So Merleau-Ponty concludes: "Transcendental subjectivity is a revealed subjectivity, revealed to itself and to others, and in that sense it is an intersubjectivity" (PP 361, 415).

With this result—that subjectivity is an intersubjectivity, that the social dimension is always already present—we have returned to our beginning, to what I took for granted at the beginning: that communication is possible. And by this return we have perhaps clarified why—not only in philosophical discussion but in every context—we take communication for granted and cannot help doing so (by the mere fact of existing) and hence are somehow justified in doing so. Perhaps we can thereby understand better what it means to say that "The end of a philosophy is the account of its beginning."

E. Part Three of the *Phenomenology of Perception*: Being-for-Itself and Being-in-the-World

i. Chapter 1. The *Cogito*

We have just now considered the question of intersubjectivity, the question of how an experience of other people is possible. The result was that as a perceptual-bodily subject I communicate with others through our common world, that consequently I am always already open to the social dimension. At the same time, we found that there is a limit to the accessibility of the other, a degree of solipsism inherent in living experience. One aspect of the other person is never accessible to me, namely, his self-consciousness, his own presence to himself.

The problem thereby raised is the following: In what sense is this presence to oneself an aspect of subjectivity? What is the character of self-consciousness? Whereas Merleau-Ponty had previously investigated the relation of the subject to things (and the natural world) and to other subjects (and the social world), his problem now becomes that of investigating the relation of the subject to itself.

Here again we find something curious about the enterprise, something curious about its beginnings. We are to investigate self-consciousness. But presumably that can only mean to become conscious of self-consciousness, to become conscious of this aspect of myself, to become conscious of my consciousness of my consciousness.

Thus the enterprise itself involves a self-consciousness of a higher order. In other words, the investigation of self-consciousness is itself an instance of self-consciousness. The investigating is itself an instance of what is being investigated. Hence, the investigation already takes what is being investigated for granted.

Merleau-Ponty's discussion of the *cogito* is in my judgment the most important chapter of the *Phenomenology of Perception*. It marks a transition of Merleau-Ponty's thought to a new level. He indicated as much at the end of the previous chapter: "These descriptions can, and must, be an occasion for us to define a comprehension and a reflection that are more radical than objective thought. To phenomenology understood as direct description, there must be added a phenomenology of phenomenology. Accordingly, we need to return to the *cogito* in order to find there a *logos* more fundamental than the one of objective thought" (PP 365, 419).

The discussion of the *cogito* raises explicitly the problems we have identified as the central ones occasioned by the retrieval of the perceptual subject: the problem of thought ("the origin of truth") and the problem of reflection. Furthermore, in connection with these we also see how the problems of language and historicity become crucial in Merleau-Ponty's work. Even more importantly, these issues lead us to the problem of philosophy itself. We come to the point at which philosophy can become a problem for itself. This chapter will provide a first indication of Merleau-Ponty's conception of the nature of philosophical interrogation and will allow us to understand the place of philosophy in relation to science and within human life as a whole. Finally, in discussing this chapter I want not only to try to understand what Merleau-Ponty says here but also to examine some of the implications that are worked out only in his later essays.

a.) The problem of self-consciousness.

Merleau-Ponty begins: "I am thinking of the Cartesian *cogito*, wanting to bring this book to a close, sensing the coolness of the paper under my hand, perceiving the trees of the boulevard through the window" (PP 369, 423).

This sentence announces practically all the themes of the chapter:

(1) The first word is "I." That is precisely the problem, the nature of the subject as subject.

(2) The I is thinking, wanting, sensing, perceiving. These are the activities of the subject that must be discussed. Merleau-Ponty will try to show how thinking, wanting, and sensing refer back to perception—more generally, to our engagement in the world—and thus to show that "All consciousness is, to some degree, perceptual consciousness" (PP 395, 452).

(3) Of all these references back to perception, the most difficult (and consequential) one to establish is that of thought. Merleau-Ponty hints how he will go about it: he is thinking, *writing*, perceiving. This suggests that language will play the mediating role, will carry thought back to perception.

(4) Merleau-Ponty is thinking of the Cartesian *cogito*. But the *cogito* is itself a thinking, so Merleau-Ponty is thinking about thinking; he is reflecting. This points to the central problem of reflection or self-consciousness.

(5) Finally, while reflecting Merleau-Ponty is *also* perceiving. This suggests that reflection is not some operation cut off from our engagement in the world. Even in reflecting, the subject is simultaneously outside himself in the world—perceiving the trees of the boulevard. And he is perceiving them by throwing his gaze toward them through a *window*: accordingly, he is not a self-enclosed windowless monad. On the contrary: "At every moment my life is delivered over to transcendent things and plays out entirely amid them" (PP 369, 423).

* * *

In the most general terms, the central problem is self-knowledge, the problem of the subject's presence to itself in reflection, in self-consciousness. More specifically, is this presence to self total? Does the subject know itself completely and with absolute certainty? Is the subject capable of absolute reflection?

Merleau-Ponty introduces the problem in a way which is quite complex and which presupposes a thorough knowledge of post-Kantian French Idealism. I want to try to approach the problem more directly.

Let us first pose the problem in immediate, "existential" terms. Suppose I make a decision. For example, I decide to have nothing more to do with a particular person. My decision has a certain motivation. I might say it is based on the fact that the person is a liar. I might say this is a fact of which I have become aware and for which I have clear evidence. In other words, I might try to remain simply objective about my decision.

I might be content with this. But then I might not—especially if someone charges that my decision is unfair. I might then reexamine my motivation and try to discover whether my decision really is based only on objective facts proving the man is a liar.

I might try to uncover other motivations and see whether perhaps my attaching such importance to his untruthfulness is not just a pretense for allowing some deeper motive to become effective. I might try to see whether perhaps even my way of interpreting the facts is not already colored by other motives. I might try to see whether my decision is really motivated not by objective facts but by jealously or my feeling of insecurity and so on.

The question is: Can I ever really resolve this matter? Can I ever be certain about my decision? Can I ever be sure of having unearthed everything which contributed to the making of the decision? Can my making of that decision ever be completely transparent to me? Or is there perhaps always the possibility that I remain to some degree ignorant of myself, concealed from myself? That is, when I *reflect* on my decision, am I able to grasp the decision and all that was involved in it with complete clarity? Am I in this respect capable of complete self-consciousness, complete knowledge of myself? Or does my decision inevitably remain ambiguous?

Let us now transpose the problem to a more strictly philosophical level. In particular, let us consider it in relation to perception so as to see what the results achieved in the *Phenomenology of Perception* allow us to conclude.

We need to begin with the Cartesian *cogito*. The *cogito* arises from Descartes's attempt at universal doubt, his attempt to suspend all beliefs, to put everything in doubt. Descartes suspends all inherited beliefs and theories, even the seemingly self-evident theories of math. He suspends belief in a world of existing things corresponding to our experience. But there is one item that proves absolutely immune to doubt, namely, his own doubt or, more generally, his own thinking, his own conscious activity.

This (the "I think") is something indubitably given. I may doubt whether the things I see do really exist independently of my seeing, but I cannot doubt that I see, cannot doubt my own activity of seeing. That is something given indubitably and with absolute clarity. In Merleau-Ponty's terms, my seeing is completely grasped by reflection, that is, in self-consciousness. I have complete self-knowledge. In reflective thought my perceptual activity is purely and totally presented, known by me. With respect to my perceptual activity I am completely transparent to myself.

We can see already that Merleau-Ponty must oppose this conception. He has argued repeatedly that perception rests on an *opaque* foundation, on an anchorage in the world which is already established and which we cannot account for. But let us push the Cartesian *cogito* one step further in order to see Merleau-Ponty's opposition more clearly.

According to Descartes, reflection can totally grasp perceptual experience. In general, however, reflection can grasp only what is within consciousness: reflection (self-consciousness) is consciousness of consciousness, and hence whatever is outside consciousness is beyond its grasp. Therefore, if perceptual experience can be completely grasped by reflection, then this experience must be an activity completely within consciousness, a purely immanent activity.

Now we can see Merleau-Ponty's opposition even better. The entire *Phenomenology of Perception* has been designed to show that perception is *not* simply an activity immanent in consciousness, that perception is not an event unfolding within an enclosed sphere of consciousness. We can see this in two general regards:

(1) The perceptual subject is not a self-enclosed spectator aloof from the world. Instead, this subject is a bodily subject and, as bodily, is anchored in the world, established in the world. As bodily, the perceptual subject is not a pure (self-enclosed) consciousness. It is itself one of those things that can be perceived in the world, though indeed it is an exceptional thing. It is a power of vision which is itself visible.

(2) Perception itself is an involvement with things, an openness to things, a dialogue with them. The perceptual subject does not merely record, from an aloof position, what parades by. Rather, the perceptual subject is one which moves in the midst of things, which traces out directions and articulations by its movement.

Perception plunges into things and follows up what the things themselves suggest. For example, my seeing of a thing follows the lines, the directions, already traced out by the pattern of lighting on the thing, that is, by the configuration of light and shadow on it.

According to Merleau-Ponty, as already mentioned: "At every moment my life is delivered over to transcendent things and plays out entirely amid them."

The subject, he says: "escapes from itself into the thing seen." Or again: "The acts of the I are of such a nature that they constantly surpass themselves; consciousness enjoys no inner retreat. Consciousness is transcendence through and through" (PP 376, 431).

The perceptual subject is a transcendence toward things. It is a being-outside-of-itself: ex-sistence. It is *être-au-monde*.

* * *

Now we can see the more general problem Merleau-Ponty must confront. The Cartesian *cogito*, self-consciousness, entails that perception is immanent activity, that the perceptual subject is self-enclosed (pure) consciousness. So if perception is *not* immanent activity, if the perceptual subject is transcendence, then this involves a denial of the Cartesian *cogito*, a denial of that self-consciousness of which Descartes spoke.

Yet this denial cannot be total, for:

(1) It belongs to the very definition of subjectivity that it can know itself, that it is capable of self-consciousness to some degree. Consciousness is by definition *for-itself*.

(2) A complete denial of self-consciousness, of reflection, would destroy the very foundation of the *Phenomenology of Perception*, since that enterprise is itself a reflective one and would be impossible if reflection were nonexistent.

(3) A complete denial of reflection would be self-contradictory in the worst sense, since such a denial could itself be made only on the basis of reflection.

Therefore, the problem is how to unite in one conception the character of consciousness as transcendence (being-in-the-world) and its character as self-consciousness (for-itself). Thus the title of the entire last part of the *Phenomenology of Perception* is: "Being-for-Itself and Being-in-the-World" (*L'être-pour-soi et l'être-au-monde*).

One expedient immediately suggests itself. There are different modes of consciousness: for example, perceptual and conceptual. Though indeed there may be no total self-consciousness at the level of perception, this does not prove that complete self-consciousness is lacking at other levels. So the task is to investigate other modes of consciousness and try to discover whether with respect to them I am capable of complete self-knowledge, total self-transparency.

b.) Inner experience.

The case of inner experience—my awareness of states of feeling such as sadness, joy, love—would seem to be different from that of perception. In inner experience it would seem that I am completely transparent to myself: if I feel sadness or love, then I am certain that I am sad and that I love. This holds regardless of the object to which my feeling is attached, therefore even if that object does not (for others or for myself at other times) in fact have the value I attribute to it. Yet such purported self-transparency of inner experience is just what Merleau-Ponty denies. He argues his case by describing "false or illusory love."

In the first place, "false love" must be distinguished from pretense at love, that is, from a case in which I deceitfully play at being in love. In this play I am not deceived; if I can really carry on the play, it is only because I hide my deceitfulness from myself. And I can hide it only if I am aware of it. In the case of false love, however, the feeling is genuinely present, I am really committed to the loved one, and *at the time* it is indistinguishable from true love.

Yet with false love, there is eventual disillusionment, and after this disillusionment I can see that beneath my supposed love there was something other than love, perhaps boredom, habit, or a likeness to someone else. Also, after the disillusionment I realize that my involvement in the supposed love was not total; parts of my life remained untouched. The supposed love was bound up only with the person I took myself to be at the time, a person I now realize was not my genuine self.

But while I was caught up in the love, it was not transparent to me, and its falsity was entirely concealed. I was not in complete possession of myself. The supposed love became transparent, and its falsity was revealed, only when it worked itself out and did so in a way that led me to a better knowledge of myself.

The result is that in inner experience, in feeling, I am no more transparent to myself than in perception. In feeling, too: "ambiguity remains, and that is why illusion is possible" (PP 379, 435). For Merleau-Ponty, just as perceptual experience is not an immanent activity within consciousness, so too love is not a mere inner condition. The evidence is that love "works itself out" in what I do, in my relation with the other. And only this reveals it for what it is.

The point is that love, rather than being a mere feeling, a mere inner condition, is a way of relating oneself to another and of doing so such that the other becomes the vehicle of one's entire relationship with the world: "Likewise, for the lover who is living it, love has no name; his love is not a thing that could be circumscribed and designated, it is not the same as the love books and diaries speak of, for it is the way he establishes his relations with the world, it is an existential signification" (PP 381, 437).

Because love is an existential signification, because it is a way we transcend ourselves toward the world, so it is, like perceptual experience, never wholly transparent to us. Merleau-Ponty concludes: "Since we are always in a situation, we are circumvented from ever being transparent to ourselves; accordingly, our contact with ourselves must remain equivocal" (PP 381, 427).

* * *

The problem of the *cogito* is the problem of self-knowledge, self-consciousness, the subject's presence to itself. The question is whether total presence to oneself, total transparency, is possible.

Merleau-Ponty's investigation of perception and of feeling has shown that in neither case is there complete transparency:

(1) Perception is not (as the *cogito* would require) a purely immanent activity, not a process within a self-enclosed sphere of consciousness untouched by things. Instead, perception "escapes from itself into the thing seen." Perception is active *transcendence* toward things.

(2) The same holds for so-called inner experience, for the awareness of what we take to be states of feeling such as love. Merleau-Ponty's most important point in this regard is that love is not a mere feeling, a mere inner condition, but rather is a way of relating oneself to the world, an existential signification. That is to say, love is a way we transcend ourselves toward the world and for this reason always harbors an opaqueness.

Thus we see that in both cases what limits the *cogito*, what makes total self-transparency impossible, is the fact that the subject is transcendence (being-outside-of-itself, existence, *être-au-monde*): "At every moment my life is delivered over to transcendent things and plays out entirely amid them."

If we generalize from these analyses we can say that the entire discussion of the *cogito* hinges on the relation between transcendence and self-consciousness. There are two general issues:

(1) By showing that a mode of consciousness essentially involves transcendence, Merleau-Ponty establishes that that mode does not permit of total self-consciousness.

(2) But self-consciousness cannot be totally denied without contradicting the very fact of the inquiry, since I could not even investigate consciousness if I had no consciousness of consciousness, no self-consciousness. Hence, on the positive side, the problem is to unify in some way self-consciousness and transcendence.

c.) The problem of thought.

There remains one general mode of consciousness to be examined with respect to the question of the *cogito*: thought. This examination and its consequences form the crux of the chapter.

Before looking at Merleau-Ponty's specific discussions, we need to see clearly what is at issue in them. What is at issue first of all is the question of the primacy of perception. We saw that this primacy actually involves three aspects: the originality, the autonomy, and the founding character of perception.

We considered how earlier discussions in the *Phenomenology of Perception* establish the first two aspects. But Merleau-Ponty has still to establish that thought is essentially founded on perceptual experience. The issue is expressed in a passage we already quoted from "The Primacy of Perception": "The perceived world is the foundation always presupposed by all rationality, all value, and all existence. This thesis does not destroy either rationality or the absolute. It only tries to bring them down to earth."

So the problem is to bring reason (thought) down to earth, to expose its essential roots, its *origination* out of perceptual experience. This is the problem of the *origin of truth*. Origination does not mean simply that at first thought has to rely on experience—for example, in the sense that concepts must be abstracted from experience but that eventually thought is able to leave perceptual experience entirely behind. Rather, thought always remains *essentially* tied to perception; its very structure involves an essential dependence on perception.

It is crucial to see what would be the consequence of bringing reason down to earth.

Merleau-Ponty wants to show that thought is essentially dependent on perception, but, as we have seen, perception involves radical transcendence. Hence, Merleau-Ponty wants to show that thought involves an essential dependence on transcendence. Yet if the very nature of thought is linked to transcendence, then even in the sphere of thought there is no pure presence to oneself. In other words, my thought, no less than my perceptual experience or my love, is somewhat opaque for me. I am never in full possession of my thought; my thinking is not presented indubitably and with absolute clarity when I reflect on it.

Thus we may say that Merleau-Ponty is launching an attack on "pure thought" ("pure reason") in two directions:

(1) against a reason which is pure in the sense of being autonomous, essentially independent of perceptual experience.

(2) against a reason which is pure in the sense of involving total self-transparency.

There are good grounds to say that the *Phenomenology of Perception*—and in particular the chapter on the *cogito*—constitutes a phenomenological critique of pure reason. But as with every such critique, one must ask eventually what Hegel asked of Kant: Is it not reason itself that carries out the critique? What guarantee is there that reason is capable of this, especially if the critique leads to a severe limiting of reason?

* * *

In general, Merleau-Ponty seeks to establish the rootedness of thought in perceptual experience by showing how language mediates between them: thought is essentially linked to language and language to perceptual experience.

There is, however, one kind of thought that is relatively independent of language—at least to the extent of being able to claim the right to invent its own purely formal, purely conventional language, namely, mathematics (or more generally, any formal science). So Merleau-Ponty argues his case first with respect to mathematical thought, specifically geometry. He takes as an example the geometrical proof of the sum of the angles of a triangle equaling 180 degrees.

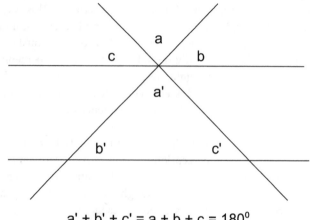

$$a' + b' + c' = a + b + c = 180^0$$

After Euclid, *Elements*:
Book I, Proposition 32.

What is involved in the thinking by which the proof is carried out? The most important point is similar to one made by Kant: the proof is not simply a result of examining the *idea* of a triangle. If I just examined the idea (the definition), I could never discover the procedure used for the proof. Instead, the proof depends essentially on the *construction* I perform. It is through this that the proof is made to emerge. In Merleau-Ponty's words:

> No definition of the triangle contains in advance all the properties that will eventually be proven as well as all the intermediaries that will have to be traversed in order to arrive at the proofs. It is possible to extend a side, to draw a parallel line through the opposite apex, to appeal to the theorem concerning parallels and their secant only if I consider the very triangle that is drawn on paper, on a blackboard, or in imagination, that is, only if I consider its physiognomy, its concrete arrangement of lines, its Gestalt. (PP 385, 441)

So what is involved here is not insight into the concept of triangle but a construction which exhibits something in intuition. Of course, I can formalize the proof. By the methods of analytic geometry I can write the proof in a way that does not refer at all to the visible diagram: for example, as a problem of the relation between series of linear equations.

But such formalization is always something subsequent; I formalize what I have already discovered intuitively: "formal thought takes its life from intuitive thought" (PP 385, 441).

So geometrical thought is not a matter of pure concepts but of constructing something in the perceptual field and of unfolding through the construction the possibilities latent in the figure: "The construction makes explicit the possibilities of the triangle, to the extent that the triangle is considered not according to its definition and as an idea, but according to its Gestalt and as a pole of my movement" (PP 386, 442).

Hence, geometrical thought depends essentially on the perceptual dimension in which there are Gestalten, configurations, for us, the dimension in which constructions and movements are possible. That is to say, our involvement as perceptual subjects in the world, our anchorage in the perceptual world, stands at the basis of geometrical thought.

Finally, it should be noted that Merleau-Ponty's argument hardly suffices to establish the general conclusion, namely, the rootedness of formal in perceptual experience. Merleau-Ponty has simply shown how this is so in the case of geometry, that particular formal science whose perceptual roots are most apparent. But there are other formal sciences where this is by no means so easy to show. An example is formal logic, which obviously has nothing to do with diagrams, or modern abstract algebra, where the mathematical object has no exemplification in perceptual experience.

* * *

Merleau-Ponty now turns to the more extensive problem of nonformal thought. He proceeds to establish the rootedness of this thought in perceptual experience by introducing the problem of language. Specifically, he tries to show, first, how speech and language involve an essential reference to perceptual life and, second, how thought is inherently linked to speech.

(1) Speech and perceptual experience.

When we first reflect on speech we tend to consider its relation to the body rather unimportant. Initially we tend to conceive speech in an abstract way, as follows:

We possess, stored away, a certain stock of words. When we want to say something (when we have an idea to express) we survey this stock mentally and choose the right words. Then, after we have the words before us mentally, we speak the words by activating certain bodily mechanisms.

So the actual sounding of the words, the involvement of the body, is unimportant. What is essential is the immanent mental activity that precedes it. So we tend to regard speech as essentially an immanent activity, the result of which may then be translated into sounds made by the body.

For Merleau-Ponty this is a hopelessly abstract account and completely misses the genuine phenomenon of speech:

A word is not an object (mental image) we call up, represent to ourselves clearly and distinctly, and then pronounce. Fundamentally, a word is a certain use of my body: "a particular modulation of my body as being-in-the-world" (PP 403, 461). I have words at my disposal the same way I have bodily movements (such as gestures) at my disposal.

Furthermore, just as I do not first decide to move my arm, then find it, and then finally move it, so likewise I do not first call up the word and then speak it. According to Merleau-Ponty: "The words and turns of phrase needed to bring my significative intention to expression recommend themselves to me . . . only by a certain style of speaking from which they arise and according to which they are organized without my having to represent them to myself" (S 88, 110–11).

In this connection Merleau-Ponty refers to the way we learn a word. We do not first have a concept and then attach a word to it. Instead, a word is "seized and appropriated": "One day I 'got the hang' of the word 'sleet,' in the same way that I learn to imitate a gesture" (PP 403, 461).

We learn what a word means by seeing it used in the context of a certain situation: "Language will become meaningful for the child when it becomes a *situation* for him" (PP 401, 459). Language is a means for taking a certain stance toward the world.

Therefore, language (speech) is essentially linked to the body and to our being-in-the-world. Thus it is linked to transcendence and so has an opaqueness. Speaking (expression) is not an activity presented to reflection with absolute clarity.

(2) Speech and thought.

Speech and thought are inseparable. Speech is not the mere clothing of thought, does not just translate ready-made thought. Rather, thought crawls along in speech and is brought to fruition only in an act of expression. The thought is acquired only when expressed. Merleau-Ponty has already presented this view in the chapter on speech, and now he elaborates it in the chapter on the *cogito* and in *Signs*.

There is indeed a secondary speech which simply communicates a thought already acquired, communicates it in the very words sustaining the thought. But this points back to an originating speech in which the thought is acquired for the first time. We use available means of expression but precisely in order to follow up (to express) a thought-intention which outstrips them. That is, in originating speech we throw the existing means of expression "out of joint" in order to say something not contained in them.

Let us consider this more closely. In originating speech, there are three "steps":

First, there is the mere thought-intention, the significative intention. But this is empty as long as it has not embodied itself (been fulfilled) in words. It is the silence behind speech: "The significative intention (even if it is subsequently to fructify in 'thoughts') is at the moment no more than a *determinate gap* to be filled by words—the excess of what I intend to say over what is being said or has already been said" (S 89, 112).

Second, there are the available significations embodied in the language I speak. The significative intention takes these up as its vehicle:

> For the speaking subject, to express is to become aware of; he does not express just for others, but also to know himself what he intends. Speech does not seek to embody a significative intention which is only *a certain gap* simply in order to recreate the same lack or privation in others, but also to know *what* there is a lack or privation of. How does it succeed in doing so? The significative intention gives itself a body and knows itself by looking for an equivalent in the system of available significations represented by the language I speak and the whole of the writings and culture I inherit. (S 90, 113)

Third, in the act of expression these available meanings are made to reveal a meaning not contained in them and to fulfill thereby my previously empty thought-intention:

> We say that a thought is expressed when the converging words intending it are numerous enough and eloquent enough to designate it unequivocally for me, its author, or for others, and in such manner that we all have the experience of its carnal presence in speech. Even though only profiles of the signification are given thematically, the fact is that once a certain point in discourse has been passed, the profiles, caught up in the movement of discourse outside of which they are nothing, suddenly contract into a single signification. And then we sense that *something has been said*—just as we perceive a thing once a minimum of sensory messages has been exceeded, even though the explanation of the thing extends as a matter of principle to infinity. (S 91, 114)

According to Merleau-Ponty, expression involves a "coherent deformation" of available meanings.

From this interrogation Merleau-Ponty concludes that expression is something opaque, "an obscure operation," an "ultimate fact." We can see this in two senses:

First, expression rests on acquired meanings, on acquired language, on an entire linguistic heritage that can never be fully thematized and made explicit. Second, expression involves a leap (not a derivation) from available meanings to new meaning. Expression is creative and as such is opaque. In expression, I leap from available meanings to new meaning just as in perception I leap from profiles to the thing itself, and the operation by which I do this is in both cases shrouded in obscurity.

Therefore, as the link of speech to perceptual experience already indicated, speaking is infested with opaqueness: "No analysis could thoroughly clarify language and array it before us like an object" (PP 391, 448).

This entails that speech is not an activity which can be made perfectly transparent by reflection. Here as elsewhere no total self-consciousness exists. Furthermore, since thought depends essentially on expression, thought also is infested with an opaqueness: complete self-transparency, complete self-consciousness, is equally impossible at the level of thought: "Accordingly, self-possession or self-coincidence is not the definition of thought; on the contrary, self-coincidence is a result of expression and is always an illusion, inasmuch as the clarity of what is acquired rests on the thoroughly obscure operation by which we have eternalized in ourselves a moment of fleeting life" (PP 389, 446).

Therefore, speech brings thought to fulfillment, brings it before me so that I possess it and know what I am thinking. Yet at the same time speech, with its obscure foundation, separates my thought from me and prevents its being perfectly transparent to me, prevents me from ever knowing completely what I am thinking. My thought outruns me.

d.) Ideas and truths.

The belief in eternal truths is powerful. There is virtually no limit to what a person will do when assured he is doing it in the name of truth. It is a belief which is perhaps as deep-seated as our belief in a world of objects existing independently of subjectivity. It seems unquestionable that Newton's laws or the truths of Euclidean geometry subsist independently of our cognitive and expressive efforts to grasp them, just as it seems unquestionable that things persist in their own independent existence in complete indifference to our acts of perceiving them.

Yet Merleau-Ponty has shown that our belief about things is not unquestionable. On the contrary, he has called radically into question this objective conception of things and the world. His inquiry has retrieved, beneath the objectified world of science and common sense, the perceptual world, that is, the world as linked to the perceptual subject in a relation of mutual envelopment. Furthermore, he has done so by bringing to light the obscure foundations on the basis of which there is a world for us, by retrieving those opaque origins we are naturally inclined to overlook. Merleau-Ponty has exposed that deception, that forgetfulness with respect to origins, which perception itself perpetrates.

His task is now to do the same in the domain of thought as regards ideas and truths. He wants to expose their opaque origins, that is, bring them down to earth, and in so doing undermine their presumed absoluteness and objectivity.

This is indeed a timely undertaking, for our century, probably more than any other, has witnessed the collapse, the relativizing, of many things which for centuries had been taken as eternal verities. For example, Newtonian physics has proved to be only a special case of much more general laws. That is, the laws of classical physics have proved to be valid only under certain very special conditions, and because of their relation to special conditions they failed to include certain relations such as those expressed in Lorenz transformations.

Likewise, Euclidean geometry, regarded as a model of eternal truth since antiquity, has come to be regarded as only one possible geometry and not even necessarily the most appropriate geometry for understanding the physical world.

So Merleau-Ponty's task is to bring truth down to earth, to expose its roots and by so doing to show the emptiness of the claim to absolute truth. In such an attempt, there is obviously a reflexive problem, a recoil of the interrogation on itself. For if thought is shown not to be absolute, then the very thought which shows this is itself nonabsolute and cannot lay claim to being an eternal verity. To pose limits to thought is to pose limits to the posing itself.

This, it seems, is the inevitable predicament in which a radically finite philosophizing finds itself. As we proceed, we shall see something of what this entails in regard to Merleau-Ponty's understanding of the character of philosophical thought.

* * *

We considered Merleau-Ponty's discussion of the problem of the *cogito* with respect to thought. The results provide a basis for confronting the problem of truth. Let us begin by summing up these results:

(1) Thought depends essentially on expression. I take possession of my thought, I fulfill my empty thought-intention, I "know" what I think, only in and through an act of expression.

(2) Expression is inherently opaque. Expression cannot be made perfectly transparent by reflection. We saw this opaqueness in two different respects. First, expression rests on acquired meanings, on a linguistic heritage which can never be made fully explicit. Second, expression involves a leap from acquired meanings to a new meaning. It is not a derivation whose course could be fully explicated. Instead, as a leap, as creative, it is inherently opaque, an "ultimate fact."

(3) Thought, as inherently linked to the obscure activity of expression, itself involves an opaqueness, a nontransparency which can never be completely eliminated. I am separated from my thought; complete self-consciousness, the *cogito* in the full sense, is impossible.

* * *

Thought is inseparably tied to expression. This implies that what is intended (an idea, a signification) in thought is also essentially linked to expression. The idea, which thought at first intends emptily, comes into my possession only at the end of an act of expression in which I have made it dwell in my language: "I say that a signification is acquired and henceforth available when I have succeeded in making it dwell in a speech apparatus which was not originally destined for it" (S 91, 114). Thus "what we call an idea is necessarily bound to acts of expression" (PP 390, 447).

If ideas are linked to expression and language and are sustained through their embodiment in language, then ideas are not supratemporal, supraspatial beings totally independent of the context in which they are thought. Instead, ideas have a history and a geography.

If ideas appear to hover above the world and outside of time, it is only because they are acquired: we take them for granted and forget their origins. "The non-temporal is the acquired" (PP 392, 450). In different terms: "expression effaces itself in favor of the expressed" (PP 401, 459), "makes itself be forgotten" (PP 401, 459).

The situation is parallel to what we found in perception: we lose ourselves in the thing perceived and forget perception. Likewise, we lose ourselves in what is expressed and forget the expression itself which first made an idea exist for us. In both cases, objective thought depends on a fundamental forgetfulness.

Merleau-Ponty carries this one step further by applying it to the question of truth. If ideas have beneath them an obscure background, if they involve a degree of opaqueness, then we never have completely transparent insight into completely self-evident truths: "Every truth of reason retains a coefficient of facticity" (PP 394, 451).

Indeed, I have an experience of truths; I experience them (for example, the law of noncontradiction) *as* self-evident. But this experience always occurs against a background of what I already believe and have already acquired. And in my experience of truth, I can never array before me, in transparent fashion, all the reasons and presuppositions involved:

> If I could bring out all the presuppositions involved in what I call my reason or my ideas at each moment, I would always find experiences that have not been made explicit, extensive contributions from the past and present, a whole "sedimented history" that not only concerns the *genesis* of my thought but also determines its *meaning*. (PP 395, 452–53)

> This experience of truth would be absolute knowledge only if we could thematize all its motives, that is, only if we ceased to be in a situation. (PP 395, 453)

So there are self-evident truths which are irresistible insofar as I take for granted a certain acquisition, a certain sedimented history: "Truth is another name for sedimentation" (S 96, 120).

All truths are, in the final analysis, situated truths.

* * *

These conceptions of thought and truth raise several issues taking us in the direction of Merleau-Ponty's later work. Let us consider four such issues:

(1) Most of Merleau-Ponty's discussion concerns the linking of thought to expression. But this is not his whole task; he also wants to trace thought back to its roots in perceptual experience. That means he must show how expression is linked to (emerges from) perceptual experience.

Indeed, Merleau-Ponty has thrown some light on this problem. He has shown that speech is essentially bodily and that the meaning of words is tied to the context of our being-in-the-world. And earlier he suggested that speech is a way of "singing the world": it captures a style, an aspect, of the world as encountered perceptually.

It remains to be shown, however, just what such a capturing involves. When an aspect is captured in speech, it is transformed: it is thematized and made explicit. It is made to exist for me in a way different from its mute presence in perceptual experience. Granted that speech has its roots in the perceptual dimension, it nevertheless represents a new achievement, a new way for meaning to exist.

So what is the character of this transformation? Merleau-Ponty says explicitly in a note to *The Visible and the Invisible*: "There remains the problem of the passage from the perceptual meaning to the linguistic meaning, from behavior to thematization. . . . Language accomplishes, by breaking the silence, what the silence wished and did not obtain" (VI 176, 229–30).

(2) Merleau-Ponty has shown that truth is always disclosed against a background of opaque acquisition, a background tacitly taken for granted: truth is sedimentation. The consequence is that truth is always situated truth, is radically historical. Even in its grasp of truth, the subject does not escape the fact that subjectivity is temporality.

Merleau-Ponty's position—that truth is always situated—has the appearance of severely restricting our cognitive possibilities. We would express this by saying that his position is relativistic; it denies us a fixed Archimedean point of absolute certainty. But in saying this we are presupposing a certain model of knowing, namely, that the most adequate knowing would be one which is absolved from all linkage to a situation and is a standpointless viewing. We devalue our own situated truth by contrasting it to a nonsituated truth.

If we set this presupposition out of action, however, then Merleau-Ponty's position can be seen in a different light. For, my being situated not only relativizes my truths but at the same time is that by which I am linked to, have access to, those things about which I seek the truth:

> Since we are all hemmed in by history, it is up to us to understand that whatever truth we may have is to be acquired not in spite of but through our historical inherence. Superficially considered, our inherence destroys all truth; considered radically, it founds a new idea of truth. As long as I cling to the ideal of an absolute spectator, of knowledge with no point of view, I can see my situation as nothing but a source of error. But if I have once recognized that through it I am grafted onto every action and all knowledge which can have a meaning for me, and that step by step it contains everything which can *exist* for me, then my contact with the social in the finitude of my situation is revealed to me as the point of origin of all truth, including scientific truth. (S 109, 137)

Thus, the fact that I am situated is not only a limitation on my capacity to discover truth but is also the guarantee, the source, of that capacity. We devalue situated truth only because we contrast it with a nonsituated truth, only because, in other words, we see it under the shadow of the absolute.

(3) Merleau-Ponty's position that truth is situated must deal with an obvious objection. We need to examine this objection in order to grasp the full force of what Merleau-Ponty is saying.

It might be contended that, however much our thinking and our experience of truth are rooted in an obscure basis that can never be made fully explicit, however much our discovery of ideas and truths is infested with facticity and historicity, nevertheless this applies only to our discovery, not to what is discovered. That is to say, over and above the obscure and situated process of discovery, the ideas and truths persist independently of that discovery.

In reply, Merleau-Ponty asks: Does this explain anything that is not already explained in the conception of truth which sees in it a relation to expression and to history? Is this not a theological prejudice rather than an explanation? He goes on: "What is this eternal truth no one possesses? What is this object expressed that nevertheless resides beyond all expression . . . ? The positing of God would not at all contribute to the elucidation of our life. Indeed we have no experience of an eternal truth or of a participation in the One; instead, we experience concrete acts of appropriation by which, in the midst of the hazards of time, we forge relations with ourselves and with others" (PP 394–95, 452).

Merleau-Ponty develops this issue in some essays in *Sense and Non-Sense* ("The Metaphysical in Man," "Faith and Good Faith"). There are two lines of development:

First, the supposition of truths subsisting in themselves is a useless hypothesis. In other words, there is no reason to suppose an absolute thought for which these truths exist—an absolute thought I would rejoin or imitate to the extent that I come to know these truths—because whether I suppose this or not makes no difference in regard to the discovery and existence of truths for me. Whether or not there is an absolute thought, my own thought is finite, and truth can come to exist for me only through my struggle for expression and insight in the face of the world and in communication with others.

In fact, it is only because I experience a certain concordance in my opinions and between myself and others that I am tempted to posit an absolute thought. But this absolute thought could provide some guarantee for my truths only if I had access to it:

> Whether there is or is not an absolute thought and in each practical problem an absolute evaluation, my own opinions, which remain capable of error no matter how rigorously I examine them, are all I have at my disposal for judging and it remains just as difficult to reach agreement with myself and with others. I can keep believing that agreement is in principle always attainable, but I have no other reason to affirm this principle than my experience of certain concordances, so that in the end whatever substance there is in my belief in the absolute is nothing but my experience of agreement with myself and with others. Recourse to an absolute foundation—when it is not useless—destroys the very thing it is supposed to found. (SN 95, 166)

This last sentence suggests a second point: recourse to an absolute is not only useless but also destructive. Merleau-Ponty is saying that the positing of an absolute thought and the supposition that I can rejoin it in contemplating eternal truths will tend to withdraw us from the genuine locus in which the discovery of truth can occur, namely, our engagement with the world and with others.

The positing of an absolute serves either to devalue all human truth or else to encourage a presumptuousness which can claim to ignore the human situation:

> If I in fact believe I am able in all evidence to rejoin the absolute principle of all thought and all evaluation, then I have the right to withdraw any judgments from the corroboration of others on condition that I have my consciousness for myself. My judgments take on a sacred character, and in particular—in the realm of the practical—I have at my disposal a plan of escape in which my actions are transfigured: the suffering I cause turns into happiness, ruse becomes reason, and I piously cause my adversaries to perish. Thus, when I place the ground of truth or morality outside ongoing experience, either I continue to hold to the probabilities it offers me (merely devalued by comparison to the ideal of absolute knowledge), or I disguise these probabilities as absolute certainties. . . . I drop the prey to catch its shadow. (SN 95, 166–67)

Merleau-Ponty concludes: "Metaphysical and moral consciousness will die upon contact with the absolute, because this very consciousness, beyond the flat world of habitual or indolent consciousness, is the living connection of myself with myself and of myself with others" (SN 95, 167).

Thus the positing of an absolute can serve to produce presumptuousness in the form of an ideology that can ignore its bonds with the human condition.

But there is also another possibility, one which Merleau-Ponty sees as a characteristic of much of Christianity: the absolute can also serve simply to withdraw us from the sphere of decision and action and thus to justify quietism: "There is always a Stoic component in the idea of God: if God exists, then perfection has already been attained outside this world; since perfection cannot be increased, there is in the strict sense nothing to do. 'My kingdom is not of this world'" (SN 174, 309).

Yet this is only one side of Christianity. On the other side, Christianity has as its peculiar virtue its rejection of the absolute God of the philosophers. Instead, it heralds "a God who takes on the human condition" (SN 96, 169).

Christianity, which Merleau-Ponty calls the "religion of the death of God," is "the most resolute negation of the conceived infinite" (SN 97, 169). Nevertheless, Merleau-Ponty charges that the consequences of the Incarnation are not followed out—"the world is not futile; there is something to be done" (SN 175, 311)—consequences that could make the Christian a revolutionary. Christianity remains ambiguous.

(4) We have noted already that Merleau-Ponty's conclusions regarding truth apply specifically to philosophical truth. So what can be said about the character of philosophical thought, granted Merleau-Ponty's position that thought and truth are radically situated, finite?

The most obvious consequence is that philosophy is not a matter of discovering (reenacting) some preexistent, subsisting (absolute) truth. On the contrary, philosophy involves bringing truth into being; thus philosophy is creation. Recall the Preface to the *Phenomenology of Perception*: "The phenomenological world is not the mere explicit expression of a preexistent being but is the founding of being; philosophy is not the reflection of a preexistent truth but, like art, is the bringing of truth into being."

This does not mean, however, that philosophy is purely creative, pure spontaneity, bound by nothing beyond itself: "Philosophy as creation, resting on itself—that cannot be the final truth" (VI 174, 227). Thought is not mere spontaneous creation because—although it is indeed no imitation of a preexistent truth—there is still a *logos* to which it is bound. But it is the *logos* not of thought but rather of the world, a Lebenswelt-*logos*: "The only preexistent *logos* is the world itself" (PP xx, xv). "At issue is a creation called forth and engendered by the Lebenswelt as operative, latent historicity which prolongs creation and bears witness to it" (VI 174, 228).

So philosophy bears witness to the world, to the *logos* of the world. Let us draw out the consequences.

First, it means that philosophy (metaphysics) does not deal with some special region of things above and beyond those dealt with by the sciences—for example, essences rather than facts: "Reflection is no longer the passage to a different order which reabsorbs the order of present things: it is first and foremost a more acute consciousness of the way in which we are rooted in them" (S 105, 131).

Furthermore, this awareness of roots is not one in which the rootedness is brought *completely* to light. That would amount to dissolving it. It is rather an awareness of our presence to the world and to others *as* nontransparent, mysterious. Recall the passage from *Sense and Non-Sense*: "Metaphysical consciousness has no other objects than those of everyday experience: this world, other people, human history, truth, culture. But instead of taking them as all settled, as consequences with no premises, and as if they were self-evident, it rediscovers their fundamental strangeness to me and the miracle of their appearing."

Second, what does this then say about the relation of philosophy to science? If philosophy cannot ensconce itself in some higher order above the sciences, if it has no other objects than just those the sciences investigate objectively, then philosophy cannot cut itself off from the sciences: "The philosopher thinks about his experience and his world. Except by decree, how could he be given the right to forget what science says about this same experience and world?" (S 102, 128).

So Merleau-Ponty says that philosophy must accept the acquisitions of science. Does this mean that philosophy is then simply the handmaid of science, that it simply lopes along behind science, systematizing or generalizing scientific conclusions? No. Science has the first word but not the last. The task of philosophy is not to systematize science but to confront the schematization and naive objectivism of science:

> Science may indeed purchase its exactness at the price of schematization. But the remedy in this case is to confront it with an integral experience, not to oppose it to philosophical knowledge come from who knows where. (S 102, 128)

> Philosophy is not a particular body of knowledge; it is the vigilance which does not let us forget the source of all knowledge. (S 110, 138)

This is to say that philosophy is the radical retrieval of origins, of the origins of all knowledge, and that its task with respect to science is to confront scientific knowledge with the very origins of such knowledge.

* * *

The entire chapter on the *cogito* is directed to the problem of the relation of the subject to itself. More specifically, Merleau-Ponty explores the presence of the subject to itself, self-awareness, self-consciousness. Still more specifically, Merleau-Ponty seeks to determine whether it is possible for the subject to have a total grasp of itself in an act of reflective thought.

We now need to draw together the results we have considered and then examine Merleau-Ponty's position.

In effect, the chapter on the *cogito* is a demonstration of the impossibility of a total grasp of the self in an act of reflective thought. We can formulate two general reasons why such a reflective grasp is not possible.

(1) For purposes of his demonstration, Merleau-Ponty distinguished three modes of consciousness: external experience (perception), inner experience (feelings such as joy and love), and thought. He then showed that the first two of these involve radical transcendence. That is, they are not immanent activities or conditions but rather are ways of being-in-the-world, ways of movement toward the world, engagement in the world. As such, they cannot be fully grasped by an act of reflective thought.

Much the same was then shown with respect to thought itself. Merleau-Ponty maintains in general that thought is linked to perception and hence to transcendence. In greater detail he shows how there is always an element of opaqueness in thought by virtue of its essential dependence on the obscure workings of expression. Because of this opaqueness, thought can never be laid out completely and with perfect clarity in an act of reflection.

Therefore, we can say with respect to all three modes of consciousness that a total reflective grasp is impossible. Of course, this is not to deny that we have some reflective grasp of these modes; it is only to say that this grasp is always incomplete, that there is always something that remains hidden from it.

(2) But there is a second issue. Merleau-Ponty has shown that thought always rests on an opaque foundation and is hence never pure. In other words, thought always harbors a mass of presuppositions tacitly taken for granted (such as those built into our language). We can never expose all that we, by virtue of being in a situation, take for granted.

Reflection is itself an act of thought, and thus it too is subject to this condition. That means reflection does not merely thematize (simply mirror) the unreflected but thematizes it *in terms of* that mass of presuppositions involved in thought. Reflection is situated. But then what guarantee do I have that reflection mirrors the unreflected without distortion?

That is to say, what guarantee do I have that my experience is the same prior to being reflected on as it is after thematization by reflective thought? What guarantee do I have that the reflection does not alter the experience reflected on? After all, I cannot compare the experience before reflection with the experience as presented to reflection, since I have access to the experience only through reflection.

In *The Visible and the Invisible*, Merleau-Ponty explicitly raises this question. Of course we have here no absolute guarantee. We have only a certain faith, a certain assurance. Specifically, this assurance is derived from perceptual experience in which a thing remains the same in moving from the periphery to the center of the perceptual field. That is, we transfer to the order of reflection the testimony of perceptual experience that when something is thematized (becomes the focus of perception) it does not undergo any change. We transfer the stability of the perceptual field to the field of reflection: "This is a massive conviction drawn from external experience, where I have indeed the assurance that the things under my eyes remain *the same* while I approach them to inspect them better. . . . We transfer this certitude to the interior" (VI 37–38, 59–60).

We need to note two points. First, what we have is a conviction, a faith, not a guaranteed certainty. Second, this indicates one way reflection is sustained by perceptual experience; our trust in reflection is derived from a certain trust at the level of perceptual experience.

* * *

In summary, there are two factors involved in the fact that a total reflective grasp is not possible:

(1) That on which we reflect—our prereflective experience—is inherently such as to escape being grasped by reflection, since that experience involves transcendence and opaqueness.

(2) Reflective thought itself is—like all thought—situated and hence dependent on a mass of unthematized presuppositions. It is no pure grasping of the prereflective but rather is a grasping of it *in terms of* this mass of presuppositions.

All of this applies to the *Phenomenology of Perception* itself, since it is a reflective interrogation. Merleau-Ponty's own work is itself situated, historical. That is to say, the truths it puts forth cannot be regarded as eternal verities. Instead, they are linked to a particular time and situation. But this would constitute a negative judgment on Merleau-Ponty's work only if we insisted on contrasting situated truth with absolute truth, only if we continued to regard human knowing in a contrast to divine knowing. If, on the other hand, we set this contrast aside, it might be said that Merleau-Ponty's work—precisely because it is linked to a particular age—is eminently capable of shedding light on that age.

* * *

Let us return to the problem of the subject's presence to itself. A complete self-presence in an act of reflection is impossible. Nevertheless, Merleau-Ponty insists that the subject is in some way genuinely—even indubitably—present to itself.

This self-presence has its locus, however, not primarily in an act of reflection but within experience itself: "I am certain of doubting because I take up such and such a thing, or even all things and my own existence, precisely as doubtful. It is in my relation with 'things' that I know myself; inner perception comes later and would be impossible unless I had made contact with my doubt by living it all the way through to its object" (PP 383, 439).

For example, when I see, I am certain that I see not because I "step back" and reflect on an act of seeing. Rather, my certainty of seeing is bound up in the seeing, in the fact that something unfolds before me in a coherent configuration and is revealed and confirmed in the course of my seeing: "The way I reassure myself that I am seeing is by actually seeing something or other. . . . Vision comes into its own, and comes to itself, in the thing seen. It is indeed essential to vision to grasp itself, and if it did not do so it would be the vision of nothing; but it is also essential that it grasp itself in a sort of ambiguity and obscurity, since it does not fully possess itself but, on the contrary, escapes from itself into the thing seen" (PP 376–77, 432).

The point is that one's presence to oneself is not something above and beyond one's presence to the world (one's transcendence). Instead, self-presence is bound up with transcendence: "It is by communicating with the world that we communicate indubitably with ourselves" (PP 424, 485).

But what is the character of this self-presence? And how is it related to, bound up with, transcendence? Here we arrive at a central problem involved in the transition from the *Phenomenology of Perception* to *The Visible and the Invisible*. In the former, Merleau-Ponty's thought on this issue moves in two directions which are not entirely compatible, as he later realized.

(1) The first direction is the one leading to the notion of a tacit *cogito*.

Presence to self is not, fundamentally, a matter of reflection. To the extent that I am in touch with myself in reflection, it is only because I am already present to myself before reflection. This fundamental self-presence is thus prereflective. Merleau-Ponty calls it the tacit *cogito*.

It is a presence to myself prior to reflection, thought, and language. It is prior to and presupposed by the spoken *cogito*. In *The Visible and the Invisible*, Merleau-Ponty identifies it with Sartre's notion of a nonthetic consciousness of self. The *Phenomenology of Perception* describes the tacit *cogito* in these terms: "Behind the spoken *cogito*, the one that has been converted into a pronouncement and into the truth proper to an essence, there is indeed a tacit *cogito*, an experience of myself by myself. But this proto-subjectivity has only an oblique purchase on itself and on the world" (PP 403–4, 462).

The tacit *cogito* is a *mute* awareness of the unity of the subject in all of its experiences. That is what Merleau-Ponty says in two passages attempting to articulate it:

To the open unity of the world there must correspond an open and indefinite unity of subjectivity. Like that of the world, the unity of the ego is invoked rather than experienced each time I carry out a perception, each time I obtain evidence, and the universal ego is the ground on which these radiant figures stand. . . . What then remains, on this side of my particular thoughts, to constitute the tacit *cogito* and the original world-project? What am I, in the last analysis, inasmuch as I can glimpse myself outside of every particular act? I am a field, I am an experience. (PP 406, 465)

Silent self-consciousness grasps itself only as a general "I think" before a confused world as the "to be thought." Any particular knowledge, even the reconquest of this general project by philosophy, requires the subject to wield powers of which he does not possess the secret and, in particular, to convert himself into a speaking subject. The tacit *cogito* is a *cogito* only when it has brought itself to expression. (PP 404, 463)

So the tacit *cogito* is a prethematic, prereflective self-awareness. It is an awareness which is virtually empty, a self-awareness only as a "generalized 'I think,'" as a field, an experience. It can become thematic and gain real content only when it finds expression for itself and thus becomes a spoken *cogito*. But then it is no longer an immediate self-presence but is rather a presence to oneself through the obscure medium of language.

(2) Is this understanding of self-presence as a tacit *cogito* satisfactory? There would seem to be another direction of thought in the *Phenomenology of Perception*, a direction not in accord with this notion of a tacit *cogito*.

Self-presence must be integrated into transcendence: "The first truth is indeed 'I think'—on condition this is understood as 'I am given to myself' only by being given over to the world" (PP 407, 466). But is this the case with the tacit *cogito*? Would it not be more correct to say that the tacit *cogito* and transcendence are correlative rather than integrated? The tacit *cogito* requires transcendence (specifically, language) in order to become a genuine *cogito*, but it is itself *prior* to transcendence.

In other words, with the tacit *cogito* does not Merleau-Ponty retain a kind of pure interiority, pure immanence, *behind* experience? But he had excluded this in his statement, quoted above, that "The acts of the I are of such a nature that they constantly surpass themselves; consciousness enjoys no inner retreat. Consciousness is transcendence through and through."

That the tacit *cogito* retains a pure interiority is confirmed in *The Visible and the Invisible*. There, Merleau-Ponty completely rejects the notion of a tacit *cogito*. In the relevant note, he begins by summarizing the notion and the thinking which led him to it in the *Phenomenology of Perception*. Then he writes:

Is this correct? What I call the tacit *cogito* is impossible. To have the idea of "thinking" (in the sense of the "thought of seeing and of feeling"), to make the "reduction," to return to immanence and to the consciousness of something, it is necessary to have words. It is by the combination of words (with their charge of sedimented significations, which are in principle capable of entering into other relations than the ones which served to form them) that I *achieve* the transcendental attitude, that I *constitute* the constitutive consciousness. (VI 171, 224–25)

The reasons he gives here are not easy to understand. What he seems to say is that the understanding of self-presence in the mode of the tacit *cogito* introduces a constituting consciousness, a consciousness prior to all the linguistic and social structures by which a world of perception, a social world, and a world of ideas are always already constituted. Thereby is introduced a purely *immanent* presence of the self to itself which is in no way *constituted* but is instead purely *constituting*.

Even to distinguish such a pure immanence, however, even to make the reduction to a dimension prior to language, is already to operate within language: "it is necessary to have words." Furthermore, Merleau-Ponty suggests that to make this reduction is to be duped by a certain presupposition built into our language and our relation to language: "Mythology of a self-consciousness to which the word 'consciousness' would refer" (VI 171, 225).

What this suggests is that self-presence is not some pure immanence prior to transcendence (a tacit awareness of the unity of experience) but rather that it is a presence to self *in* the movement of transcendence.

Merleau-Ponty says in a note to *The Visible and the Invisible*: "The true philosophy = apprehend what makes the leaving of oneself be a retiring into oneself, and vice versa. Grasp this chiasm, this reversal. That is the mind" (VI 199, 252).

ii. Part Three of the *Phenomenology of Perception*: Chapter 2. Temporality

A remarkable statement stands very near the beginning of the chapter on temporality: "There are no principal and subordinate problems: all problems are concentric" (PP 410, 469).

We might say this is so because, in a sense, there is for Merleau-Ponty only *one* problem: the problem of subjectivity or, better, the problem of being-in-the-world, that is, the problem of bringing to light and articulating that whole in which the subject and the world adhere to each other.

Merleau-Ponty's statement suggests that this problem is not to be solved by piecing together the solutions to various subordinate problems. It is not as though we could solve the problems of space, movement, sexuality, intersubjectivity, and self-consciousness and then simply bring these together to form a total conception of subjectivity. Instead, all these problems are concentric: with each of them the *whole* of subjectivity is, in a sense, traced out.

On the other hand, this does not mean that Merleau-Ponty first formulates, implicitly or explicitly, a general conception of subjectivity and then applies it to these particular problems. Rather, each of them serves for gaining access to subjectivity as a whole. Merleau-Ponty makes this clear in introducing his analysis of time: "To analyze time is not to deduce the consequences of a preestablished concept of subjectivity; it is to gain access, through time, to the concrete structure of subjectivity" (PP 410, 469).

So the analysis of time is a means of gaining access to subjectivity as a whole. Of course, there are other means, but the analysis of time has a special importance because it brings the subject as a whole to light more primordially. In terms of Merleau-Ponty's image: if subjectivity is itself the center around which all problems circle, then the problem of time is perhaps the circle which is closest to the center.

Thus the analysis of time will allow us to gain a final conclusive view of the conception of subjectivity that emerges from the *Phenomenology of Perception*.

*   *   *

Merleau-Ponty's problem is the relation of time to subjectivity. Without following Merleau-Ponty's polemics, let us try to see how he posed the problem.

Suppose time is a sequence of moments:

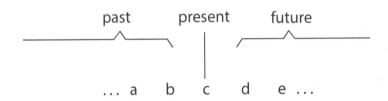

Then how is the subject related to time? We say that the subject is *in* one of these moments, namely, the present. But that is not enough. The subject is not confined to the present but also has access to the past and future, is open to the past and future. That means the past and future must be connected to the present. But how? Presumably through a synthetic activity of the subject, binding together the moments of time. Thus it seems that the subject constitutes the connectedness of time.

This has a further consequence: in order for the subject to connect the moments of time, the subject must itself not be *in* any of those moments. That is, the subject must be situated at a point external to all moments so as to be able to have the moments before it and bind them together:

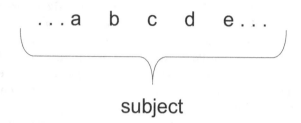

The diagram above shows the subject outside all of the moments of time, which are represented by a series (a, b, c, d, e) trailing off in two directions, that of the more and more remote past and the one of the more and more remote future. Such a subject, external to the entire series, could indeed synthesize time. But the result is that the subject has no present. The subject is equally close and equally distant from all moments and thus can have no sense of past, present, and future. All moments are reduced to a uniform level. Thus such a subject could have no genuine time-consciousness.

Versus such a conception, Merleau-Ponty says: "Time exists for me because I have a present" (PP 424, 484). So his problem is this: how can the subject be situated in the present and yet have access to the past and future?

In general, it is possible if the unfolding of time (its connectedness) is not something the subject accomplishes (constitutes) but rather is something the subject lives through, something the subject is. Thus Merleau-Ponty proposes that the *subject is time*. Let us try to see what this means in the concrete.

Merleau-Ponty attempts to understand the subject's openness to the past and future by introducing the character of the subject as transcendence. The subject is not a self-enclosed consciousness. Instead, in the present the subject has a "field of presence." That means the subject *is* a presence to the world. It is through my presence to the world that "I make contact with time" (PP 416, 475). What does that mean? How is it that in my presence to the world I make contact with the past and the future?

In perceiving a thing, the profile presently given has trailing behind it the profiles previously given. Also the present profile points ahead to other profiles still to be given. This takes place without any explicit effort on my part. I do not explicitly relate past and future profiles to the present one. Instead, this network of intentions (retentions and protentions) is laid out in my very way of being present to the perceptual field: "They emanate, not from a central ego, but, as it were, from my perceptual field itself, which trails behind itself its horizon of retentions and which bites into the future by way of its protentions" (PP 416, 476).

So in my presence to the perceptual field the past is retained. It is not something explicitly remembered but rather something transparently visible through the retentions borne along in my relation to the world. There is a network of intentions linking the past and future to the present:

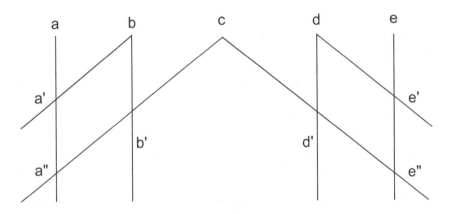

This network of intentions is not something I constitute; retention is not equivalent to explicit memory, nor protention to explicit anticipation. This network is not the outcome of some synthetic activity on my part. Instead, it is something borne along, something unfolding, in my presence to the world: "The 'synthesis' of time is a synthesis of transition; this synthesis is the very movement of a self-unfolding life. The only way to carry out the synthesis is to live that life, for there is no extrinsic ground of time: it is time itself that bears itself and casts itself forth" (PP 423, 484).

So time is not a sequence of discrete moments which would need to be linked together in some way by some synthetic activity. It is rather a "unitary thrust" (PP 423, 484). That is to say, the connectedness of time is inherent in the very upsurge of a new present: "The new present is the passage of a future into the present and the passage of the former present into the past: it is with a unitary motion that time, from one end to the other, advances" (PP 419, 479).

Time is not a succession of moments but is rather a phenomenon of flow: "We do not have here a manifold of combined phenomena but, instead, a unitary phenomenon of flow" (PP 419, 479). Merleau-Ponty expounds:

> What there is is not a present, then another present that succeeds the first in being; nor is there even a present with perspectives on the past and future, followed by another present in which those perspectives would be overthrown, such that one and the same spectator would be required to carry out the synthesis of the successive perspectives. On the contrary, there is a single, self-confirming time that can lead nothing into existence without having already founded it as an approaching present and as a past to come. Thus what there is is a time that establishes itself at a single stroke. (PP 421, 481)

Earlier we said that the subject *is* time. Merleau-Ponty states explicitly: "Time must be understood as the subject, the subject as time" (PP 422, 483). We can now see something of what that means. Time is not a sequence of moments over against the subject, such that the subject is either contained in one moment or is outside all moments so as to link them together. Instead, time is a phenomenon of flow, an unfolding of the network of intentions in the presence of the subject to the world, the unfolding of a life.

Let us try to see more precisely what the identity of the subject and time means. Time involves certain characteristic features or structures: for example, a retentional structure. Likewise, subjectivity involves certain features or structures: for example, transcendence, self-consciousness. To say that the subject and time are identical is to say that the essential structures involved in both are identical. So we need to lay out the two sets of essential structures and see how they correspond.

What are the essential structures of subjectivity? The chapter on temporality concludes with a survey of these as they come to light in the *Phenomenology of Perception*:

(1) Subjectivity is being-in-the-world.

"We discovered, at the heart of the subject itself, the presence of the world, such that the subject could no longer be understood as synthetic activity but, instead, had to be grasped as ek-stasis" (PP 429, 490). That is, the subject is not cut off over against the world but, on the contrary, is an active transcending toward the world. Otherwise expressed, what is fundamental is neither subject nor world (as isolated terms) but rather the intertwining of both in transcendence: "The world is inseparable from the subject—specifically, inseparable from a subject that is nothing other than the projection of the world. And the subject is inseparable from the world—specifically, inseparable from a world the subject itself projects. The subject is being-in-the-world, and the world remains 'subjective,' because the texture and articulations of the world are predelineated by the subject's movement of transcendence" (PP 430, 491–92).

Or again, Merleau-Ponty says that the subject and object are "two moments abstracted out from the unitary structure that is *presence*" (PP 430, 492).

(2) Subjectivity involves facticity.

This means that "our open and personal existence is founded on a first stratum of acquired, fixed existence" (PP 432, 493–94). The subject is always rooted in an obscure ground of primal acquisition or sedimentation. The *Phenomenology of Perception* has especially shown how the body is the vehicle of this acquisition. But the acquired is not limited to the bodily and perceptual. Even at the level of thought, we operate on the basis of a primal acquisition of meaning (especially as embodied in language).

(3) Subjectivity is self-consciousness.

As we saw, this self-consciousness is not that of the Cartesian *cogito*, not a matter of reflection above and beyond the level of experience. Instead, it is a self-consciousness which is wholly bound up in the movement of transcendence. Thus it is a self-presence which *is* only in the subject's presence to the world, as already quoted: "It is by communicating with the world that we communicate indubitably with ourselves."

Now we need to see how these three structures correspond to those of temporality.

(1) We learned that to say the subject is transcendence is to say that it is engaged in a perpetual flight beyond itself, outside of itself: "The acts of the I are of such a nature that they constantly surpass themselves; consciousness enjoys no inner retreat. Consciousness is transcendence through and through." But this character also expresses the essence of time. Time is a "unitary thrust," a movement of the present beyond itself into the future: "Subjectivity is not immobile self-identity; subjectivity must, by its very essence and just in order to be subjectivity, go out of itself and open itself to an Other, precisely as time must do in order to be time" (PP 426, 487).

(2) The primal acquisition involves the retention of the past, the retention of something already established. That is, it involves the carrying over of what is past into the present, a carrying over which is beneath the level of our personal acts and which serves to found those acts.

But this structure—the entering of the past into the present at a level beneath that of personal acts—is precisely the structure of retention, by which the past is retained nonthematically in the present. Therefore, the passage quoted earlier about our open and personal existence concludes as follows: "Our open and personal existence is founded on a first stratum of acquired, fixed existence. But it could not be otherwise, if we are temporality, since the dialectic of the already acquired and the yet to come is constitutive of time" (PP 432, 493–94).

(3) The subject is self-conscious, but its self-consciousness is bound up in transcendence.

How is this structure exemplified in the structure of time? In my continual passage into the future a series of past moments is retained. Thus, in my present experience I have a grasp on my past experience; in other words, in my present (the passage to the future) I have a grasp on myself as past. So Merleau-Ponty says: "It is essential to time not only to be factual time, time that flows, but also to be time that knows itself, since the explosion or dehiscence of the present toward a future is the archetypical *relation of self to self*" (PP 426, 487).

Furthermore, since this network of intentions is bound up with my presence to the world, the presence of myself to myself is also a presence bound up with transcendence. Therefore, the structure of self-consciousness is not only mirrored in the structure of temporality but is further elucidated by it. Thus we see how, in general, a presence to self can be inscribed within transcendence.

But this is to claim (as was said at the beginning) that to analyze time is to gain access, through time, to the concrete structure of subjectivity.

Subjectivity	Temporality
1. Being-in-the-world (Transcendence)	Time as thrust toward the future
2. Facticity (Primal acquisition)	Retention of the past
3. Self-consciousness	Retention of the past in thrust toward the future

iii. Part Three of the *Phenomenology of Perception*: Chapter 3. Freedom

Karl Marx said: "You cannot do away with philosophy without fulfilling it." Accordingly, the fulfillment of philosophy is, in some sense, its destruction.

For Merleau-Ponty, who agrees here with Marx, this destruction takes a peculiar form: it is the destruction of philosophy as something isolated, cut loose from its existential roots. In "Marxism and Philosophy," Merleau-Ponty says: "Philosophy fulfills itself by doing away with itself as isolated philosophy" (SN 133, 236–37). Or again: "Knowledge finds itself put back into the totality of human praxis and, as it were, given ballast by it" (SN 134, 237).

A principal aim of Merleau-Ponty's discussion of freedom is to pose this question of praxis and of the relation of philosophy to praxis. Let us outline his argument regarding freedom:

(1) It might first be argued that the subject is not a thing; hence it is not determined by objective causality: "For one to be determined by something from the outside, one would have to be a thing oneself" (PP 434, 496). But if there can be no objective determinism, then presumably the subject is absolutely free: "One cannot be 'a little free'" (PP 435, 497).

Yet how could this absolute freedom be understood? Are there not obviously obstacles limiting my freedom? Here Merleau-Ponty revisits a famous Sartrian analysis.

I want to climb a mountain. As I ascend, I come upon a huge rock I cannot scale. Is this not an obstacle to my freedom? Sartre answers, "No." The rock is not an external obstacle that limits my freedom. Instead, the unclimbable rock is unclimbable only within the framework of my project of climbing. In itself it is neither climbable nor unclimbable.

In other words, it is my own free project which confers this meaning on the rock, hence it is an obstacle posited by freedom itself. So freedom, rather than being limited by something external, remains absolute.

(2) Merleau-Ponty assumes a critical stance toward the concept of absolute freedom. He insists that such a freedom destroys the possibility of free action, since it is "on this side" of all action. It is not a freedom which has to be exercised but one which is already acquired prior to all action: "Freedom would be on this side of all action, and in no case could it be declared: 'This is where freedom emerges.' The reason is that free action can show itself only against a background of life which was not free or was less free. It can be insisted that freedom is everywhere; but then it is also nowhere" (PP 437, 499).

The problem then is to understand how freedom can be limited without there being some kind of causal determinism. The *Phenomenology of Perception* has provided a means for such an understanding. We have seen that the subject is primordially rooted, anchored, in the (natural and social) world and that the subject's personal existence, hence its free acts, are always linked to (presuppose) this anonymous anchorage.

So prior to my free act, something is already laid down, established, assumed. There is always already a certain field within which my freedom is exercised.

(3) Application to Sartre's analysis. Indeed the character of being unclimbable is conferred on the rock by a human presence. It can be unclimbable only for a subject. Given the project of climbing, however, one rock will appear as an obstacle and another as a means—and this is not determined by my free project.

That is, when I undertake my project of climbing, it becomes possible in general for things to be obstacles or means. But my project does not determine whether *a given rock* will be an obstacle or a means. Instead, my project takes place within the scope of a prior project through which the world and things are already structured:

> There is indeed a genuine distinction between my explicit intentions—e.g., my current project of climbing these mountains—and my general intentions which gauge my virtual purchase on my surroundings. . . . As a thinking subject, I can at will situate myself on Sirius or on the surface of the earth, but beneath this subject there is something like a natural ego that does not leave its terrestrial situation and that ceaselessly delineates absolute values. . . . Inasmuch as I have hands, feet, a body, a world, I am the bearer of intentions which I have not deliberately chosen and which therefore endow my surroundings with characteristics I have not chosen. (PP 439–40, 502)

(4) Merleau-Ponty now extends the same conclusion to the subject's relation to society and history. He considers the phenomenon of class-consciousness. How do I come to be conscious of myself as an exploited worker and hence become a revolutionary?

It is neither as a causal result of objective conditions (determinism) nor simply a conscious decision, judgment, suddenly made. Instead, I first exist as a worker in the sense of being caught up in a certain way of dealing with the world and with others. Thus class is, first of all, something lived: "For class is neither simply observed nor peremptorily decreed; like the appointed order of the capitalistic apparatus, and like a revolution, class, before being thought, is first lived in the guise of an obsessive presence, a possibility, an enigma, a myth" (PP 446, 509–10).

Merleau-Ponty generalizes to all social-historical phenomena: "If I could in fact make myself a worker or a bourgeois through an absolute fiat, if, more generally, nothing solicited my freedom, then history would admit of no structure, we would see no events delineating themselves in it, and anything could arise out of anything else. . . . History would never be heading anywhere, and, even if we considered a very brief period of time, we could never say that events were plotting some result" (PP 449, 512).

So, for Merleau-Ponty, the individual subject is neither the object of history (history is no alien force, externally determining man) nor is the individual the subject of history, making those decisions (which determine history) from some point of view outside history, independently of history: "We do indeed confer on history its meaning, always provided history proposes that meaning to us. The *Sinn-gebung* is not only centrifugal, and that is why the historical subject is not simply the individual. There is an exchange between generalized existence and individual existence, each of them receives and each gives. . . . Freedom can modify the meaning of history only by appropriating, in such a way as to 'ease' it in a new direction, the meaning history itself *offers* at any moment" (PP 450, 513).

(5) Therefore, in relation to both the world and history, what we find is a free act which takes up something already established. What we find is a freedom that is always situated: "We choose our world, and the world chooses us" (PP 454, 518). Furthermore, "we could not possibly delimit what is contributed by the situation and what is contributed by freedom" (PP 453, 517).

Because our freedom is situated, we are never absolutely free and "The choice we make of our life always takes place on the basis of certain givens" (PP 455, 519).

(6) These ideas are essential for understanding Merleau-Ponty's political thought and his relation to Marxism.

In "Marxism and Philosophy," Merleau-Ponty speaks of the idea of "a politics which is not created ex nihilo in the minds of individuals but is prepared and worked out in history" (SN 105, 184). That is, to engage in politics requires a certain response to what history offers at the moment. Merleau-Ponty says that history "rejects the men and the institutions that do not respond to existing problems" (SN 105, 184–85). Politics involves taking up and transforming what the historical situation offers. And in particular it does not involve simply applying ideas already thought out independently of the historical situation.

That is, the transition from philosophy to praxis is not a mere application of abstract ideas to another sphere. It is this that Merleau-Ponty has in mind when he says a politics of consciousness is impossible.

(7) Finally, we can take this even further: likewise, a *philosophy* of consciousness is impossible. Philosophy, too, like political action, is exercised always from out of a situation. Philosophy too has its roots, its historical anchorage.

That is, the philosopher cannot take his stance *above* history, society, and the world. As we already quoted from *In Praise of Philosophy*: "Philosophy cannot be a tête-à-tête of the philosopher with the truth. It cannot be a judgment given from on high regarding life, the world, history, as if the philosopher were not part of it."

That means the philosopher does not disengage himself from his situation so as to formulate eternal abstract principles to be externally applied to concrete situations: "Should I make this promise? Should I risk my life for so little? Should I sacrifice my own freedom in order to save freedom itself? These questions cannot be answered at the level of theory" (PP 456, 520).

Philosophy does not place us beyond our situation and give us "once and for all" a means of dealing with situations. Rather, philosophy leads us to see the situation more clearly; it serves to recall us to our rootedness. Philosophy is the return to origins. According to Merleau-Ponty, in words we quoted very early on: "Whether it is a matter of things or historical situations, philosophy has no other function than to allow us to see these things and situations accurately, and so it is true that philosophy consummates itself by destroying itself—as isolated philosophy."

Merleau-Ponty concludes: "But here we must fall silent, for only the hero lives, all the way to the end, his relations to human beings and to the world, and it is not proper for anyone else to speak in his name" (PP 456, 520).

Editor's Afterword

THIS VOLUME OF John Sallis's *Collected Writings* presents his lectures at Duquesne University on the philosophy of Maurice Merleau-Ponty. The text is based primarily on Sallis's two-semester graduate lecture course in the school year 1970–71. The course was announced in the registrar's catalog as follows: "Philosophy 649–650. Merleau-Ponty. Six credit hours. Beyond realism and idealism. The functions of the phenomenal body. The structures of the 'lived' world. Spatiality, temporality, language, sexuality. Perception and knowledge."

Sallis had also offered a two-semester course on Merleau-Ponty at Duquesne in 1968–69, and the present volume incorporates supplementary material from those lectures. The later course was a thorough reworking of the earlier one. It also greatly expanded the treatment of *The Visible and the Invisible* and condensed the discussion of *The Structure of Behavior*. Most of the supplementary material thus relates to *The Structure of Behavior*. The engagement with *The Visible and the Invisible* in the later course has already been published and is omitted here (see footnote 1, p. 124).

Little editorial intervention was required in preparing these notes for publication. They are written in a clear longhand and are nearly always expressed in full sentences. Because the text incorporates two separate courses, I did at times need to integrate, but in every case Sallis had specified which sections of the earlier course were to be interpolated where. Also, I verified all the references to Merleau-Ponty's works, inserted as part of the front matter the list of abbreviations to which the references are keyed, and provided the page numbers of the original French. In the notes, the direct quotations of the English translation often amount only to the first word or two and the last, with ellipses in between. While filling in the entire quotation, I occasionally modified the published translation for the sake of a more literal rendering. Lastly, although Sallis's notes display few colloquialisms, some changes in phraseology and diction were required, as might be expected in the transition from oral delivery to printed page.

I thank John Sallis for entrusting these lectures to me, and for very helpful comments on the penultimate version of the entire text I am grateful to one of his current graduate assistants, my daughter Christine Rojcewicz.

Richard Rojcewicz

Index

adaptation, 25
affectivity, 87–88
afferent system, 19, 21, 28
ambiguity, 2, 5, 7–8, 66, 89, 97, 104, 120, 123, 139, 156
amovable forms, 33
anatomical (circuits, structures, devices), 14–16, 20–22, 25, 29
animals, 17, 20, 35, 43
anonymity, as pre-personal, bodily existence, 78, 85, 99, 101, 102, 105, 122; as the presence others in a cultural object, 126–31
aphasia, 91
association, 65–67, 70, 80, 88, 92, 127
atomicity, 15–18, 23–26, 65–66
attention, 18, 65, 68–70

behaviorism, 14, 24, 33, 38
being-in-the-world, 34, 58–59, 104, 109; the body as vehicle of, 77, 85, 105; as pre-conscious, 77; body image as a way of, 80; as projective function, 81–83; speech rooted in, 92–93, 144, 149; as bodily anchorage, 77, 120; as finite subjectivity, 128, 158, 162; and solipsism, 133; as transcendent consciousness, 138, 164; inner experience as a way of, 154
Bergson, 2, 35
bestowal of meaning, as bodily operation, 86–87, 90
biology, 39, 43, 52
blindness, 100
the body, as lived (phenomenal, subjectivized), 12, 76, 78, 122, 128; as active in experience, 14; not a blind mechanism, 20, 45; as the presence of a constitutive history, 52; as always there, invariable in perspective, 76; as vehicle of being-

in-the-world, 77, 85, 105; as anonymous, an inborn complex, 78; as distinctively spatial, 79–81; as a sexed being, 85–89; as a bestower of meaning, 86; as expression, 90–94, 143–46; as forming a system with the perceived world, 96–97; as the subject of synthesis, 102–105, 114–23; the body of the other person, 127–30
body image, 80,
brain, 19, 25, 27–31, 77, 79, 83. *See* central nervous system

categorial attitude, 28, 43
causal thought, 23–24, 75–79, 97, 104, 122, 165
central nervous system, central sector, 19, 25, 27, 31
chaos, of sensations, 31, 67; of irrationality, 71, 72
chiasm, 158
Christianity, 152
class, class-consciousness, 4, 165–66
cogito (the "I think"), 33, 41, 46, 123, 124, 134–38, 140–41, 144, 147, 153, 157. *See also* tacit *cogito*
Collège de France, 2
color, 98–99, 116–18; shift depending on light, 30, 117; inherent motor meaning of, 98
communication, with others, 4, 125, 130–33; of the senses, 100–101
communism, 3–4
conditioning, 25, 88. *See also* Pavlov
consciousness, metaphysical, 1, 152; and nature, 11–14; pure, 12, 14, 33–34, 54, 95, 104, 128; as an original yet rooted structure, 14, 34; and behavior, 33–34; transcendental but not absolute, 34; as intentionality, 40–41, 48; as self-consciousness, 41–42, 50, 134–38, 163; situated, 44–45, 85, 95; intellectual versus

JOHN SALLIS is Frederick J. Adelmann Professor of Philosophy at Boston College. He is author of more than twenty books, including *Light Traces*, *The Return of Nature*, and *The Figure of Nature*. From 1966 to 1983, Sallis was Professor of Philosophy at Duquesne University; the lecture courses he offered there on Merleau-Ponty form the basis for the text presented herein.

RICHARD ROJCEWICZ was a graduate student in philosophy at Duquesne University in the early 1970s and was thereby privileged to attend many of John Sallis's lecture courses. Rojcewicz is a prolific translator of Husserl and Heidegger and is author of *The Gods and Technology: A Reading of Heidegger*.

CPSIA information can be obtained
at www.ICGtesting.com
Printed in the USA
BVHW040933160223
658528BV00015B/117